Rumble Strip

Canada 150

The WindWord Group
Publishing & Media
Suite 200, 100 Bull Street, Savannah, GA 31401 USA
www.windwordgroup.com

Copyright © 2018 Gail Hulnick
All Rights Reserved.

No part of this book may be scanned, reproduced or distributed in printed or electronic form without permission.

ISBN-10: 1-947527-99-1
ISBN-13: 978-1-947527-99-7

Library of Congress Control number: 2017918271

Please contact the publisher regarding large-quantity book purchases, interviews, or speaking requests
email admin@windwordgroup.com

Printed in the United States of America

Rumble Strip

Canada 150

GAIL HULNICK

The WindWord Group
Publishing & Media

RUMBLE STRIP CANADA 150

DEDICATION

For David. He knows why

CONTENTS

Introduction		9
Chapter One	Newfoundland	18
Chapter Two	Nova Scotia	34
Chapter Three	Prince Edward Island	48
Chapter Four	New Brunswick	59
Chapter Five	Québec	68
Chapter Six	Ontario	78
Chapter Seven	Manitoba	88
Chapter Eight	Saskatchewan	96
Chapter Nine	Alberta	109
Chapter Ten	British Columbia	121
Chapter Eleven	Reflections	135
Playlist		139
About the Author		146
About Rumble Strip Books		147

Introduction

"That is a road trip I have always wanted to do." The young man serving our dinner in the Moncton restaurant was the first person I'd told about our cross-Canada journey since we crossed the border from the U.S. (Actually, I guess, he was the second person because first was the border services agency officer at St. Stephen, New Brunswick, just across the line from Calais, Maine. Technically, though, we hadn't actually crossed a border until after he waved us through.)

Alex was the waiter's name, and when he came back with our crab cakes, he wanted to hear more.

"What's the route you're taking?"

That's r-oo-t, not r-owww-t.

"We're going to North Sydney in Nova Scotia to take the ferry across to Newfoundland, then to St. John's and to Mile Zero. That's our starting point, and then we drive west till we get to Vancouver Island," I explained.

"Awesome. I'm going to do that someday. How far will that be?"

"Almost eight thousand kilometers. In three weeks, give or take."

A little later, after I heard him serving desserts at the next table, using flawless French, I asked him if he was from Québec.

"No, I'm from right here in Moncton," he said. "We're officially bilingual, and if you grow up here you speak French and English."

That was a surprise to me, even though I am a Canadian citizen and, until three years ago, a Canadian resident. It was the first of dozens of surprises I stumbled over during the three weeks on the road—and for my money, exactly the sort of reason you head out on an epic road trip. Find out what you don't know.

This cross-Canada road trip was both a realization and a celebration—the realization of a lifelong dream and the celebration of 2017, a very special year for the country where I was born.

Canada is one hundred fifty years old. Someday I may be. On the news this morning, I saw a report about a woman who is 111 years old and says her Fountain of Youth contains whiskey, one tot a night. She didn't say it was a tot, but it looked like a wee one, there in her glass, barely covering the bottom. (Maybe she was half or three-quarters of the way through it, though.) The life span for humans (in the easy countries) just continues to climb and climb—it's not beyond possibility that someone gets to one hundred and fifty years in my lifetime.

But if I want to celebrate a one hundred fiftieth birthday right now, it has to be a country, not a person. In 1867, in Charlottetown, Prince Edward Island, Canada, the fathers of Confederation did the paperwork that led to the creation of a new nation. No question, there's been much discussing, debating, and voting on proposals over the years since then, and we've passed many milestones. But if you're going to find an excuse for a party (or a vehicular escape) the founding of a country is a good one.

This book's title, Rumble Strip, refers to the grooves in the pavement at the side or middle of a highway that are there to wake you up if you've drifted too far over to the shoulder or out of your lane. It also works to slow you down, sometimes. Either way, it usually serves to make you more alert. To make you take a look around.

I hit a rumble strip, metaphorically, with my move to the United States a few years ago. Henry Miller wrote that one's destination is never a place, but rather a new way of looking at things. This is part of what I was after with this road trip. In addition to the bragging rights and the fulfillment of a longtime dream, I was interested in returning with a new way of looking at Canada, at my nationality, and at my new country of residence, the United States. Kahlil Gibran, in his poem "Friendship IXX," has a wonderful turn of phrase about distance and contrast and realization: "…as the mountain to the climber is clearer from the plain." Canada and the United States are both my mountains and my plains.

I started planning this trip earlier this year. If you are getting impatient with the circling around the subject and are the type who prefers a cut-to-the-chase style, then skip over the Introduction and get right to Chapter One. (Or Chapter Ten, if you want to know how it comes out in the end.) I'll save you the trouble and give it away. Yes, I did complete a road trip right to the west coast of the country.

If you are the type who reads Tables of Contents, you know there is a Chapter Eleven. (Wait, what? Somebody goes bankrupt?) No, not that kind of Chapter Eleven. Although the cost of this trip was not nothing, it didn't threaten to run me off the road. This Chapter Eleven is an overview—of the country, my road trip, travel, those three weeks, and so forth. It's everything that didn't fit in anywhere else, kind of like a blooper reel or the deleted scenes in a director's cut.

My ride on this road trip was an indigo 2001 Chrysler Sebring convertible. I specify "indigo" rather than blue or dark blue because it is another of my goals to own a car in each color of the rainbow.

(Not all at once, one at a time. Stop raising the bar!)

Red, orange, yellow, green, blue, indigo, violet. I have done red, orange (sort of a copper color, actually), green, and blue. Is indigo actually a separate color, or is it just dark blue? This is an interesting argument, and I could go on about it this for pages and pages. But it's far too soon, in the introduction of a book like this, to get into it. Let's save it for one of the interminable miles on the road in northern Ontario when we're north of Lake Superior and the next town feels like more miles away than I can count.

Are we there yet, are we there yet? Are. We. There. Yet.

We can also have a debate then about the metric system and whether I should be using kilometers rather than miles. And a debate about the spelling of 'kilometer'.

My time frame was up to three weeks. My budget was not low and not unlimited. I have a companion who provided many of the best lines in this book. I will use them shamelessly, because he said that I could. He says he wants his role in these pages to be like the neighbor behind the fence or the mother in the back bedroom on the American TV shows *Home Improvement* and *Big Bang Theory* or like the driver on the British TV show about cars, *Top Gear*—anonymous but superior. It's not quite a copy of the driver character because that one says nothing and this one says a lot, frequently. But it's close. I could also use 'this one' or 'we' or 'he says', as Miss Hathaway does. (More about her later.) I will use 'the Zig' or just 'Zig' as a nickname for him most of the time.

And that brings us to how to spell this new name. If I am in the U.S., I say Zee-eye-gee. If I'm in Canada, it's Zed-eye-gee. It's a sure giveaway about your early years and your education, that pronunciation of the last letter of the alphabet. It's not the only clue—if you say toque, eh?, or which way to the bathroom?—you're Canadian. If you're searching for the restroom, you're American.

The United States of America has been my home for the past few years, as I mentioned. This would have been quite a different road trip if it were happening in the eighties or nineties, when I had no residential basis of comparison for countries other than Canada. This drive across Canada, then, was not about a traveler discovering an unfamiliar land (although there were elements of that). It was about a citizen and a former resident returning with a goal in mind.

I was born in Alberta, attended junior high school in Manitoba, high school in Ontario, then university in Toronto, Edmonton, and Vancouver. (No, I didn't get booted out of school after school; life just kept on changing.) My working life began with television reporting jobs in Ontario and Alberta, and then flowed west to Vancouver, British Columbia, where I was host of the CBC Radio morning programme The Early Edition for six years and the noon programme Almanac for two years. These are news and current affairs shows that cover everything from politics to business to entertainment to the arts to sports. My job was to interview the guests, read the news, report the weather, and do the time checks. It was a blast—and that's a good thing because the work day often started at 4:30 a.m.

By the way, Canadians like that extra 'me' on the spelling of 'program'. Actually, that used to be the case, but lately we are dropping some of the more European or British distinctions. Canadians still write 'colour' not 'color', 'theatre' not 'theater', and 'centre' not 'center'. This creates a dilemma for me—which spelling style to use for this book? After dithering for months, I've finally come down in favor of the American style because although it's about Canada, it's being published in the U.S.

You might also be interested to know that in Canada it is 'grey' not 'gray', 'cosy' not 'cozy', 'draught' not 'draft', 'mould' not 'mold', 'plough' not 'plow', 'cheque' not 'check', 'liquorice' not 'licorice', and 'kerb' not 'curb'. Then again, you might not, and you might be thinking "get on with it!" All right, here we go. (In Canada, 'all right'; in the U.S., 'alright'.)

That's enough of that, I won't do any more. I will just tell you that my plan is to drive across Canada in two to three weeks, taking in the easternmost point (Cape Spear), using the Trans-Canada Highway (mostly) and starting at Mile Zero in St. John's in Newfoundland and Labrador.

Is this the only province, state, or country in the world to have an 'and' in its name? One of very few, I thought; at first, the only other I could think of was Turks and Caicos in the Caribbean. But a little assistance in Online Land gave me Trinidad and Tobago, Bosnia and Herzegovinia, the UK and Northern Ireland, Antigua and Barbuda, St. Kitts and Nevis, St. Vincent and the Grenadines, plus Sao Tome and Principe.

There is also more than one Mile Zero. Both the city of St. John's, capital of Newfoundland and Labrador on Canada's east coast, and the city of Victoria, capital of British Columbia on Canada's west coast, have a Mile Zero, so that regardless of which side you use to start, you are starting at the beginning.

(Never mind the irony of starting at a Mile Zero in a country that measures road distance in kilometers. Much more ranting about that later.)

How did this happen?

It's a long story with lots of twists and turns, but the essential point is that highway naming and numbering is a matter for provinces to decide, not the federal government, and so you have plenty of differing opinions showing up on a road map. It also has to do with the timing of road construction, and with Terry Fox and his epic goal, to run across Canada—more about that later, too.

When you get to the end, whichever end that is, you will have gone a distance of 7,821 kilometers, which is 4,860 miles. Again, this is a bit blurry (and no doubt very annoying to those of you who prefer precision in your measurements). It depends on a bunch of things. The two most important, to my mind, are whether you include the water distances taken on ferries when your car isn't actually driving but it is moving, and whether you count all the way across Vancouver Island to Tofino or stop the odometer at Victoria on the east coast of the island.

There are yet more ways to answer the question "How long is Canada, coast to coast?" If you measure from Cape Spear, the easternmost point of Canada and of North America, to the Yukon–Alaska border, you've got 5,514 kilometers; if you look at Cape Race, N.L. (that's Newfoundland and Labrador) in the east and Tofino on Vancouver Island in the west, it's 7,831.5 kilometers; if you're on a bicycle, doing a ride called The Crossing, it's 6,521 kilometers.

Also the Trans-Canada Highway isn't the only one to traverse the entire country east to west. You could choose to bear to the right (and northerly) just west of Brandon, Manitoba and take Highway 16, the Yellowhead Highway, through Saskatchewan and Alberta. You'd see Saskatoon then. If the Canadian rock group The Guess Who's playlist is a major part of your sense of the country, then missing this road would make you feel cheated. You'd also miss Edmonton, the capital of Alberta, and Jasper, the jewel of the Canadian Rockies. Carrying on heading west through British Columbia, you can either take 16 to 97, or 16 to 5 to 1, or 1 all the way west, or 3, closer to the U.S. border. I'm told that's just the big picture and that there are actually more than sixty ways to get across B.C. by smaller roads.

Looking to eastern decisions, where you choose to insert the province of Prince Edward Island on your journey is a matter of opinion, too. Should it come before or after Nova Scotia? Before or after New Brunswick? Or maybe before or after Québec, given its location just east and only a little bit south of the Gaspé Peninsula?

I am going east to west because that's the direction my ancestors took. Some (actually, 50 percent) of my grandparents emigrated to Canada from Ireland and Russia and headed west in search of survival and who knows what else. The others were already here but not by many generations and, again, they migrated toward the west.

I'm putting P.E.I. in just before New Brunswick. Totally arbitrary.

Canada is made up of ten provinces and three territories. Up to now, I have lived in four of the thirteen. This may be as good as it gets, since I find myself hanging out a shingle in the U.S. now.

Living is one thing, but passing through is another. You can accomplish the second one much more easily and in less time. I've heard much difference of opinion on what qualifies as truly visiting a destination. Does it count if you land at an airport just for refueling? Can you count that country if you get off the plane and buy something to eat in the airport? Is it an actual visit if you leave the airport and look around the city a little? Or do you have to spend at least twenty-four hours there? Do you have to sleep there, or does a wakeful twenty-four hours count? If you fall asleep while sitting on a bench in an airport waiting for a flight, does that count as sleeping there and visiting the country?

I have traveled in six provinces so far. Not even half of the thirteen provinces and territories. I am ashamed. My excuses are lack of funds and excess of obligations elsewhere. I also have always had a sense of 'time to get around to that later' that is as vast as Canada.

I think they call it procrastination.

But now I am old and in a hurry. I want to see as much of Canada (and every other country) as I can.

This trip focuses east to west but, of course, there is an entire other dimension to consider. Canada is just as vast north to south, with many more experiences to uncover. That will be the scope of another trip.

To get to the starting point, I had to get myself, my car, and the Zig out to Mile Zero in St. John's. To do that, we left Savannah, Georgia, and drove north on I-95 in the eastern U.S., through Georgia, South Carolina, North Carolina, Virginia, Maryland, Pennsylvania, New Jersey, New York, Connecticut, Rhode Island, Massachusetts, New Hampshire, and Maine.

Once the Canadian event was underway, I would be travelling about 7,800 kilometers. Altogether, including the U.S. leg, this trip would be about 10,000 kilometers. That's a quarter of the way around the globe.

Really?!

Well, that's what Zig says, and he does well at this math business. The earth's circumference is 40,075 kilometers. A quarter of that is 10,000-ish kilometers, and that's what we're doing.

It was summer, a good choice for a driving tour of Canada. You have to think about this even in the southern sections of the country. Summer: sunny, warm, and easy. Winter: read up on frostbite. I've been on a lot of highways, in different countries and in different conditions, but there's something about driving right across Canada that falls into the 'trip of a lifetime' category for me. I didn't want anything to turn it from being (mostly) a lot of fun into a grit-your-teeth-and-tough-it-out experience. Driving it in February would do that. I've done lots of winter driving in Canada, through whiteouts that left me parked at the side of the highway waiting it out, and through blizzards that filled the ditches with vehicles and drivers who didn't quite conquer the snow and ice. It's an adventure.

Maybe I'll try that for my second cross-Canada drive. On this first one, I'm going for the best weather conditions possible and a drive that fosters reflection and thought, rather than simple survival. Driving in Canada when there isn't a blizzard or an ice storm is pleasure, not danger.

Even when there is a blizzard or an ice storm, it's an experience worth having, though. I'm usually the one in the car who is pointing out that this is easier to take than a monsoon in India or a hurricane in the Caribbean. I'm sorry, but most of our problems today in North America wouldn't slow down an explorer or a pioneer for even five minutes. Call me naïve or just too positive, but the glass is half full and the level is rising.

A drive across Canada is not that far and is not that difficult to do, summer or winter. While not quite as well-paved and laced with freeways, secondary highways, and side roads as the U.S., the country is most definitely first-world, and any problems you encounter will be in that category.

The ride is especially pleasant in a convertible, with the speakers cranked up high. I designed a playlist of Canadian music that helped carry us coast to coast; you can find the details at the back of this book and can listen along on Spotify.com.

Just be careful not to encounter or startle a moose, as about half a million roadside signs will warn you along the highways.

How many roadside signs, exactly? I don't know and I won't be looking that up, using two or more sources for verification. This book has no footnotes and no index, in case you're looking.

Now, back to the moose ... The moose is one of Canada's native animals, a massive mammal with an impressive rack of antlers. The full-grown bull can run as high as 1,500 pounds, and if you run into one, you won't be going far after that. Trucks that traverse roads known to be on the moose's regular route are often equipped with a piece of equipment called a moose catcher. (It is also called an 'elk pusher', a 'cow catcher', or a 'bull bar'. The technical term is 'grille guard'.) They are made of steel, aluminum or stainless steel and cost anywhere from $1,800 to $6,800. They offer protection to the grille, hood, and engine, for when you collide with a moose, and a menacing, tough-guy appearance for the days when you don't.

I had no grille guard on my convertible, and the idea of colliding with a moose was right up there with my worst nightmare of coming up from a scuba adventure to find the dive boat gone.

Yet, as we got ready to drive across Canada, seeing a moose was one of the highlights I was anticipating.

GAIL HULNICK

Chapter One

NEWFOUNDLAND

The Rock

I will stop beating around the bush (not an easy thing to do in the Canadian wilderness) and tell you that I did not see a moose while going through Newfoundland. This expedition was devoid of wildlife, pretty much, except for what we encountered in a few pubs here and there. On previous Canadian journeys, I've seen Rocky Mountain goats and sheep, bears, beavers, and lynx, but this time I had only one brief sighting of a moose. In a province to be named later.

Newfoundland and Labrador form Canada's easternmost province, with the Newfoundland part to the east and separated by a body of water (called the Strait of Belle Isle) from the Labrador part, which is on the same land mass as Québec. It seems strange to those of us who grew up learning that Newfoundland joined the Canadian Confederation in 1949 and was its own province. It was the one you didn't include if you were talking about the Maritime provinces, but did if you were talking about the Atlantic provinces. They were all islands—how does Labrador fit into that?

But if I look at the whole Canadian map on the world atlas, with the various regions and provinces highlighted in different colors, I must now concede Newfoundland and Labrador *do* make sense, forming a sort of continuous backslash, a logical clump of two land masses, no weirder than any other—than, say, Vancouver Island and British Columbia, or Washington State and Alaska, for that matter. There are sound historical reasons for all of those inclusions and exclusions, but they are quite complex. Maybe I'll get around to discussing all those reasons in detail eventually, but right now that feels boring.

Newfoundland is isolated, idiosyncratic, and proud. I had never been there but, over the years, at school and at work, I've met many people from that part of Canada and, without exception, each one left me looking forward to an opportunity to visit there one day. Newfoundlanders are fun-loving, creative, and witty.

I was so excited about beginning this cross-Canada trip! As St. Augustine wrote so long ago, "The world is a book and those who do not travel read only one page." Today was to be the official beginning, starting at Mile Zero in downtown St. John's, pointing my nose west and south for an exploration of my home and native land. The world's biggest producer of canola and second biggest of oats, according to the United Nations, Canada is also one of the most well-educated countries in the world and the second 'most-admired', after Switzerland, in a U.S. News and World Report survey. Newfoundland and Labrador is known as the location of Signal Hill in St. John's, where Marconi received the first transatlantic wireless message in 1901 and engineered the birth of today's communication age. It is also the namesake of a large and spirited dog breed. It joined Confederation in 1949. The population in 2016 was 528,448. Thank you (and please support) Wikipedia.

Twelve hours ago I woke up on board the ferry. Cabin 8234. Times were not good. The floor was pitching and rolling, along with my stomach, which up until then had been feeling pretty good, thanks to a delicious seafood dinner I'd enjoyed in the onboard restaurant. I tried deep breathing and relaxing, then picked up a Julian Barnes novel, struggling to pretend that I was somewhere other than on a stretch of open water that would take sixteen hours to cross.

Depending on which cabin you book, you could have four bunks, a view to the outside, and your own bathroom to escape to or use to take a shower. The mattress was a bit hard but I fell asleep quickly. Too bad I couldn't stay that way.

As I lay awake waiting for the dawn, I felt I was safe but I found myself thinking from time to time "why am I here?", "why am I doing this?", and "I really don't like this". I was calmer in the morning, but it was a long night.

The weather was not particularly bad; they cancel the crossings when it is. But this bit of wave action was enough for me. I was awake from 2:30 to 4:00 a.m., not actually sick, but close. I heard later from one of the other passengers that she'd gone looking for seasickness medicine in the ferry's shop but there was none. No information on whether that was because they didn't stock it or had had so much demand they were sold out. I was glad to get up and go the café area for a coffee and a muffin once they opened up around 7:00 a.m.

The morning was a foggy one. All I could see was a curtain of damp, hazy mist that looked as though it had been hung just inches from the portholes. Quite a change from last night's spectacular sunset, which had drawn dozens of passengers out to the deck for almost an hour.

I had my morning coffee and muffin just a few tables away from a young man who had not registered for one of the cabins. He had obviously passed the night sleeping, or trying to, on one of the upholstered benches that lined the floating café walls, despite the numerous signs telling people that this was against the rules. At night this same area is the bar and the location for the live entertainment, which featured a comedian who doubled as the DJ. Multi-tasking is a very Canadian thing. The space is named Colours—a bit of wit, given the foggy, cloudy conditions. It looked like a disco, with lights twinkling in the ceiling and bright primary colors in the upholstery for the chairs and benches.

Would I do it again? Yes! But it would be easier the second time, knowing what to expect.

The big benefit was that I was going to land quite close to St. John's and the car was with me. I will be able to say we drove across Canada east to west in my car with no diversions to airports. Next time (and there will be a next time!) I might fly and stay longer on The Rock, but for this time, the ferry crossing experience and the drive east to west will be perfect.

The cost was lower, too—$745 CAD for a return ferry ticket from North Sydney to Placentia, sixteen hours, and then coming back from Port aux Basques to North Sydney on Saturday, six hours' crossing time. The private cabin one way added another $400 for two of us. The airfare and rental car option would have been about $1,900.

As Zig looked over the Newfoundland map, and I guzzled very good coffee, a motorcycle rider we'd met yesterday joined us in the café.

"Did you sleep well?" I asked.

"Not really," Jon said. "I didn't bother with a cabin and thought I'd just sleep sitting up in one of the chairs by the window. But it was cold."

He didn't seem like the sort who was skimping on the expenses, and as we chatted it became clear that he wasn't. He was an enthusiastic rider from Texas who had adapted his bike and equipped it with a custom-built sidecar that drew crowds and admiring comments. (We'd seen that happen in the lineup while we waited to board.) Jon just ate up the miles; he told us he'd done forty-eight states in nine-and-a-half days once. Uh huh. I was born at night but I wasn't born *last* night.

"I might have some trouble getting home on time this time, though," he said.

"What's your deadline?" I wanted to know.

"I have to be home by mid-September to take my wife to Germany and northern Spain," he answered.

"She doesn't come along on your motorbike trips?" Zig asked.

He shook his head. "Not her thing. And now, I'm behind on my schedule because I just spent four days in Antigonish waiting for a replacement for a tire that blew. They had to do a special order."

"Is there much to do in Antigonish?" Zig asked.

Jon smiled. "It's not bad."

"Where do you stay there?"

"I actually look for churchyards in most places where I stop," he said, looking every bit like the man who could pay for the five-star if he wanted to. "I pull in behind a church and put up my tent. It's quiet and nobody disturbs me."

"If they're religious, they're probably afraid they'll be punished if they do."

We all laughed and Jon went off in search of the next group to become recipients of his brief friendship on this trip. Once we docked in Newfoundland, he said, he was headed to Cape Spear, to touch a foot on the easternmost spot on the North American continent, then north and west across Newfoundland toward Labrador.

I saw a lot of motorcycle riders on this trip, many of them with gray hair and joints that didn't quite do what they did when they were thirty. A lot of the motorbikes were designed for comfort, with wide seats, three wheels, and sometimes, armrests that reached all the way around the back for the passenger. When I asked Jon about these, he said they were a big help for the older person in back who might be lulled by the road vibration into an unplanned nap, risking an unpleasant meeting with the pavement.

For me, a road trip across the country in a convertible is enough adventure at this point. Motorcycles are for a nice Sunday afternoon drive, not too far and not too long. But—never say never.

I wondered about the source of the name Labrador. Is it French in origin, perhaps related to 'bras d'or' like the lakes in Nova Scotia? According to the online source I checked later in a St. John's hotel (no Wi-Fi onboard the ferry), it is Portuguese, after an explorer named Lavrador who explored the region in 1498–99. Boundary disputes run through the history of Québec, Labrador, and Newfoundland like TV commercials run through a Super Bowl game. In 2001, the province officially changed its name to Newfoundland and Labrador, with the aid of a constitutional amendment. People with land claims still dispute the borders. Stay tuned for further developments.

Driving from the ferry after it docked about 10:30 a.m., we passed Cape St. Mary's, supposed to be a great spot for watching puffins, dolphins, and sometimes whales. Next time. Also maybe next time: the Irish Loop, a drive along the coast featuring shamrocks on the signs to show the way.

I did quite a bit of advance planning (yeah, I know, probably the most redundant phrase in the English language). But, hey, it's a big country and I didn't catch or make a note of everything. I did not know, for example, that puffins are such a big deal in Newfoundland; next time I go there, I will be prepared.

The time zone is thirty minutes later than the Atlantic Time Zone because of Newfoundland's location and because it was a separate "dominion" when the time zones were established. It is exactly three and a half hours from Greenwich, where mean time is situated. About fifty-five years ago, there was an attempt to bring Newfoundland into clock-step with the other provinces, but it failed.

The ferry unloading rules insisted we weren't allowed to go down to our vehicle until after the boat docked. People lined up along the stairs, then there was a crush and a rush to get down to the vehicle decks. During unloading, our car was positioned directly down from the tilting ramp, completely by chance. The workers put the ramp down, then motioned us to drive down it and off the ferry. We were the first, after the hundreds of motorcycles and then the cyclists (there were only two of them). Fun!

I took a few minutes to consider the pros and cons of a cycling trip, the way I had thought through a motorcycle ride earlier that morning. Man, I don't think so. The hills, the unpredictable weather, the hard work. If you cycle across Canada, you are truly a road warrior, and I salute you.

Not for me, thanks.

Our destination that morning was Cape Spear, the easternmost point of Canada and of North America and the official starting point of our journey west. It was a two-hour drive from Placentia to St. John's, after the ferry docked, a distance of 134.5 kilometers. A few scrubby trees and many signs reading 'watch for moose', but mostly I was seeing lots of nuthin'.

The Newfoundland homeowners and businesses had many Canadian flags displayed, probably thanks to the spirit of celebration of the 150th anniversary. Many of the business names were quite funny—the sense of humor is as ever-present and as essential here as rain gear most of the year. My favorite was a bed and breakfast named "No Charge for the View".

So, tourism was one way to make the rent. I also saw lots of signs for wineries. This was another surprise—I had not known that many grapes grew on The Rock. And the wineries are among the best in Canada, it turns out.

Every place you visit has its own naming conventions and here it was 'pond', used frequently. Fergus Pond, Western Gull Pond, Ocean Pond. The landscape looked like the glaciers just retreated last month, with rocks and boulders strewn about the fields we passed. I noticed a mountain peak that looked like the curl of a wave. Awesome.

This drive was very easy in summer and our weather was superb, but it was only two-and-half days. And of course, winter would be a very different story. At this time of year, purple lupins covered almost every bit of roadside, along with blue flag iris, and showy lady's slipper orchids.

The cliffs above the bright blue ocean waters near Cape Spear were amazing. As the province's website pointed out, if you stood there with your back to the road and the parking lot, there was nothing before you until Ireland. We toured a lighthouse that has been there since 1836 and read historical markers about the role the place played in defending North America during the Second World War.

We drove down from Cape Spear into St. John's, in search of Mile Zero, and actually learned about several. One is at the Railway Coastal Museum on the waterfront and is Mile Zero for The Great Trail, a recreational hiking and biking trail that is the longest in the world. Another is at the memorial to Terry Fox's Marathon of Hope, just near the foot of Signal Hill, and a third can be found at Logy Bay Road, near Middle Cove Beach, where the Trans-Canada actually ends.

There is also a Mile One Centre, an arena and recreational complex in St. John's. As to the issue of having a 'mile' zero in a country that measures distance in kilometers, I learned in St. John's that because construction on the highway across the country was started in 1950 and finished in 1971, when Canada still used miles, 'Mile' is the right word to use. Canada didn't switch to the metric system and the kilometer measurement until 1977, and so tradition and good sense dictate the name should continue to be 'Mile' Zero. If you disagree, write your own book.

Downtown St. John's is quite modern-looking, although dotted with historic Victorian houses. These are the iconic 'jellybean row houses' and you can see them, brightly painted in the primary colors of jellybeans, all over Newfoundland. You find a particular concentration of them downtown, though, on Gower, Duckworth, and Cathedral Streets. The story goes that when the fishermen were done painting their boats, any paint left over went on the houses. It takes a lot of work to maintain color like that in a climate like this, and the effort is worth it.

Water Street is a charming stretch of shops, restaurants, and pubs. I saw a lot of buskers playing live music on the street, most of it with an Irish flavor, featuring pan flutes, accordions, and drums.

Traveling along Water Street a few more kilometers brought us to the Terry Fox memorial park, and another Mile Zero. Terry is a Canadian hero who began a cross-country run in 1980 to raise funds to research and fight the disease that had claimed one of his legs and would eventually take his life as a very young man. I remember doing telephone interviews with him from our radio studio in Edmonton that spring and summer, and it was always a moving and inspirational segment. He started in St. John's in April, running a marathon a day. By September, he had conquered the Atlantic provinces, Québec, and most of Ontario. But, later that month, cancer was found to have returned to his body and he had to pause and return to his home in British Columbia for treatment. He was not able to continue the run and he died the next year, in 1981.

Since that time, millions of Canadians have taken up his challenge and every year in September they run to raise funds for cancer research. By mid-2017, over seven hundred million dollars had been raised in Terry's name.

This memorial park had a statue, panels telling his story, and a lovely wall with the inscription "I just wish people would realize that anything is possible if you try, dreams are made if you try."

As we drove through the countryside earlier in the day, I noticed that the place-naming style included a lot of 'ponds' and 'brooks'. In the city of St. John's it is 'hills'. We saw Church Hill and Cathedral Hill, for example. The streets meander rather than follow a grid, like those all over New England, where what were cow paths once upon a time became roads, then streets.

After our tour of St. John's, we stopped overnight at a hotel on the outskirts of town, catching up on the sleep we'd missed out on during the ferry ride.

The next morning, we left the city in a light drizzle. Then the clouds lifted to show off a robin's egg blue sky with fluffy gray clouds. The highway across the province has been cut through rock that has to be seen to be believed. It would be 212 kilometers to Gander, the halfway point in the day's drive. It would take about seven hours total, and at the end of the day we would be in Corner Brook, having driven the Trans-Canada Highway right across Newfoundland from east to west.

You could also go south to north or drive the perimeter, but that's the goal for another journey and another time. That route would take you up north to the place near the Titanic sinking (to the east), and near the Viking settlement (to the west). I spent a little while discussing the possibility of a detour with the Zig, but he pointed out that if we changed the plan every twelve hours, we would never finish this cross-country journey.

What a road-building feat it was, to cut a highway through these rocks! It's a rough landscape, and you have a sense that this is what it would have looked like since the dawn of time. Some of the road is quite bumpy in stretches. I saw many signs warning that this is moose and bear country, although the local wildlife didn't make any appearances for me. It was an easy, scenic drive, but can you imagine what it must be like in winter?

We pulled off the highway into a hamlet named Come by Chance. I would have stopped for the name alone, but also, I remembered it was often featured in the news as a prime example of the impact of the death of the cod fishery in Newfoundland. There were only 298 people living there now, according to the roadside sign, and there was not much but houses. No sign of any commerce.

It was in Come by Chance that we first noticed the wooden boxes at the end of every driveway or near a porch. Each was about two feet by three feet (that's about two-and-a-half square meters, in metric measurement, which Canada uses—as does the majority of the world). A long chain was looped around one end. Later I noticed them all over the Atlantic provinces. What were they? Containers for sand or salt in the winter? No, the spaces between the wooden slats made them poor candidates for holding those things in. A place to put things you want to keep away from wildlife or the neighbor's dogs? No, same reason.

I found out on inquiring later that they are for garbage bags, to prevent them from blowing away in one of the countless winter gusts. Cans or even large carts won't do the trick because the wind will turn those into projectiles.

Terra Nova National Park was next on the route. Large sections of roadway, like other areas of the national parks we drove through on this trip, were under construction; the road quality in the national parks was noticeably better in almost every province. Although it seems that the occupation of flag person is now completely gender-neutral, Terra Nova was the only place where I saw someone wearing leopard-patterned tights under her orange-and-yellow construction jacket.

The day's drive covered a bleak, empty stretch of Canada. If you enjoy isolation and that sense of frontier, you'll find it here. I saw very few towns, hundreds of miles of muskeg (Algonquian for 'grassy bog'), hundreds of moose warning signs, and thousands of garden lupines. This wildflower is a dominant feature of the hills and meadows, along with the sheep laurel and the Labrador tea. The explosions of purple, pink, and white blossoms were unexpected and absolutely gorgeous, particularly in the places where they seem to be growing out of sheer rock.

I also saw many miles of moose fence. The moose fence was designed to keep the massive animals off the highways and out of danger. Looking something like chicken wire fences but sturdier, they lined the roads, broken by occasional gates, which open in only one direction. People can pass through but the moose can't.

We passed a lookout dedicated to former Newfoundland Premier Joey Smallwood, set up near Gambo, where he was born. He was the politician who brought Newfoundland into Confederation. I never interviewed Joey Smallwood during my time as a television reporter or as a CBC Radio morning show host, but I do remember John Crosbie, another Newfoundland politician, very clearly. John ran for the leadership of the federal Progressive Conservative Party in 1983 after a long career in Newfoundland politics and then a number of years as a Member of Parliament in Canada's capital city, Ottawa. He served in the cabinets of Prime Ministers Joe Clark and Brian Mulroney. He also served as Lieutenant Governor of Newfoundland and Labrador. He had the lilting accent and the wicked sense of humor of many people from Newfoundland, and regardless of what you thought of his politics, as an interviewer you were on the edge of your seat during live-to-air conversations with him, the seven-second delay button ready to go at all times.

Besides outrageous and outspoken politicians, Newfoundland is known for arts and culture, with music groups Great Big Sea and Figgy Duff, actors Gordon Pinsent and Robert Joy, comedians Rick Mercer and Mary Walsh, writers Michael Winter, Lynn Coady, and Wayne Johnston.

It's also famous as the location nearest the iceberg that destroyed the Titanic, and the spot where airplanes were grounded during the 9-11 emergency, an event that led to the recent Broadway hit *Come from Away*. The city of Gander was once the busiest airport in North America, in the days when planes couldn't make it all the way across the Atlantic without refueling.

This road was incredibly bumpy—not really news, in Newfoundland. Potholes in Newfoundland are as common as highway billboards in Florida. I also saw a lot of transmission line workers, building new lines—good work! But not nearly as many road workers, repairing the potholes, and they would have been a welcome sight.

Our destination the second night was Corner Brook. Just before we reached the city limits, about seven kilometers east, we saw signs leading to Marble Mountain, a ski area that didn't have much happening in August but no doubt would be a completely different story in the winter. According to Wikipedia, it gets more snow, on average, than Mont Tremblant in Québec, a far more famous ski and snowboard destination.

That night, we stayed at a little inn on the main street of Corner Brook that featured a restaurant called the Crown and Moose. Framed photographs of royalty decorated the walls, along with the occasional picture of a large, antlered mammal. We took a walk through the downtown on what must be one of the prized balmy summer evenings, taking note of the public art—a mural showing a Newfoundland dog—and parking meters decorated with crocheted bracelets or necklaces (depending on whether you think a parking meter has an arm or a neck).

The next morning was the jump from Corner Brook to Port aux Basques on the southwest coast, where we were to catch a shorter ferry back to North Sydney, Nova Scotia, which we'd left two-and-a-half days ago. We had covered 850 kilometers of Newfoundland and Labrador. It was nowhere near all of it, and none of the Labrador section, but I was satisfied, and ready for Nova Scotia.

The ferry trip back to Nova Scotia was only eight hours. The day was foggy and drizzly but, inside the boat, all was comfy. I had a nice fish and chips lunch and, since there was no Wi-Fi, I saw many people's faces and heard conversations that probably would not have been happening had people had the opportunity to stare down at their phones. Some of the conversations were quite political. Many Canadians are very fearful and critical of the U.S. these days, and their opinions of the president, while not particularly positive since 1963, are notably negative right now. Many of the travelers were

Newfoundlanders getting to and from the mainland, but many others were tourists, vacationers, and older people finished with daily work and preoccupied with collecting experiences and world knowledge. I overheard two retired couples comparing notes, and it had a strong tinge of competition. These were probably the same sort of couples who took note of the quality of one another's lawn grass or yard fencing or furniture and kept on trying to have the 'best'.

"Did you see the northern and western areas of the province? Gros Morne National Park. L'Anse aux Meadows, where the Vikings were?"

"Oh, yes, we were there fifteen days."

"Well, we were there eighteen days."

"We had nothing but sunshine the whole time. And we saw thousands of puffins."

"We saw thousands of puffins and a pod of whales passing this close to shore."

"We saw thousands of puffins, two pods of whales . . . and a black bear."

"We saw thousands of puffins, three species of whales, a bear . . . and a moose!"

Okay, you win.

I also heard serious comfort-campers from Florida, Massachusetts, and Michigan discussing the best ways of seeing Newfoundland and Labrador. The consensus seemed to be that you leave the RV back on the mainland, unhook the small car (or SUV) that you are towing, and use it to come over on the ferry, then stay in a B and B.

I was starting to get the hang of the accent, deloyt-ful, royt? I have always had the unconscious habit of taking on some of the cadences and slang of whatever place I'm in for more than forty-eight hours—only some of them, though, which weighs against any possible career I might have as a voiceover actor or dialect coach. I'll be right in the middle of channeling a soft Southern voice that's as believable as biscuits, barbecue, and moonlight-through-the-pines—then all of a sudden a Canadian 'hoosse' will land and people will wonder what I'm talkin' a-boat. Or I might be relaxing with Boston friends and telling stories about the time I went to the pahk with my fahthah, when a sem-ee comes rolling around the corner and drowns me out with the sound of squealing brakes.

Much as I might try to imitate the musical sound of an Irish person or the posh tones of an English public school graduate, I fail exactly when I try. But if I just hang out and talk with people for a while, the accent thing starts to happen.

I'm cautious with it though; while it does help with fitting in and avoiding sounding like an outsider to be circled with caution and suspicion, you have to be very specific and you can't over-generalize about people's voices or accents. Different provinces express different accents (and slang, habits, and clothing styles). If you go around using the accents in the depiction of Canadian 'hosers' (that's hoe-zers, not hoo-zers) from eighties TV as your paradigm of Canadian voices, you should be aware that you might sound right for the Ottawa Valley or perhaps Regina, Saskatchewan, but like blends or combinations of anything, they're a little bit of each, not the full expression of either. It's like calling something an American accent: is that Georgia? Texas? New Jersey?

Then, you can go beyond regions and get into occupations: California surfer sounds very different from Boston taxi driver; Texas cowboy sounds very different from New York financier.

Be aware, particularly, if the local or regional accent contains seeds of its origins in original settlers or ancestors. Newfoundlanders sound a bit like the Irish, in one way—but in another, not at all. They are unique, and the more you hear and learn, the more you realize there is to know.

I have to go back one day. To Newfoundland, you understand. Not New Fund Lund. Maybe next time, I'll have more luck in spotting wildlife.

For now, I carry on to a place where some long-ago lyricist wrote "the birds were singing on every tree."

Some famous people born in, educated in, housed or claimed by Newfoundland and Labrador?
Actor Gordon Pinsent. Reality TV show star Shannon Tweed. Writer Gwynne Dyer. Explorer Leif Erikson.

Hockey player and sports announcer Howie Meeker.

What to see next time?
When we drove off the ferry at Argentia in the east, there were signs to an Irish Loop Highway that looked intriguing but just wasn't in the plan. I'd stop for that next time. Also for the Cape St. Mary's Ecological Reserve, a twenty-four-square-mile bird sanctuary that features astounding cliffs and one of the biggest seabird colonies in the world, just fifteen kilometers or so along a well-paved road from the main highway. It's easy to miss it in your excitement about getting off the ferry and away from the long water-ride, not to mention the pull of getting to St. John's and to Cape Spear, but I heard from many travelers that it was a high point of their trip to Newfoundland and Labrador. Puffins and gannets in the tens of thousands. The walk from the visitors' center is about half a mile and well worth it, they say, even on a mauzy, foggy day. If it's foggy or raining, so much the better, for the impact when you see a rock covered in birds as the fog rolls in and out. It's also one of the best spots to see whales in the wild without going out on a boat.

I would also go back and travel farther north to see the ancient ruins of Viking settlements at L'Anse aux Meadows.

What to see more of?
Moose.

Music performances. I saw only one and I was impressed. It was at a tiny pub in Corner Brook, and the guy gave us everything from Johnny Cash to Gordon Lightfoot to Cat Stevens to Brad Roberts to something of his own.

Bottles of Iceberg Beer.

What to see less of?
Muskeg. Yes, I get that I have a better chance of seeing a moose in a muskeg landscape than in downtown Toronto but, truly, when I am riding across it for hours and hours

at a time and you try to tell me there's not too much of it? Well . . . g'wan.

Surprises?
The artistry in the way the houses are integrated with the hillsides, the waterfronts, and just about every feature of the landscape. Yes, I'd seen photos of the brightly colored jellybean houses, but none do them justice.

The distance from the mainland. It is not a minor ferry ride.

The cuisine. Yes, you can get exceptional seafood, but you don't have to eat it at every meal, and the menus are varied and entertaining. Don't miss the blueberry crisp.

Chapter Two

NOVA SCOTIA

"Will you ever heave a sigh or a wish for me?"

This line, from the folk song "Farewell to Nova Scotia" (covered by many singers and belonging to all), expresses the longing of a wanderer far from home, inspired by memories of "the sea-bound coast" and the birds singing on every tree.

Nova Scotia also inspired the music of one of my all-time favorite singers, Stan Rogers. If you enjoy folk or roots music and you're not familiar with his work, give yourself a gift and look him up.

I rolled into North Sydney, Nova Scotia from the deck of the MV Highlanders ferry with Stan's song "Northwest Passage" playing on the soundtrack in my head. It's been there ever since I first heard it in the early eighties when Stan was playing small venues throughout Canada and radio shows like ours in Edmonton, Alberta. The song was once suggested as an alternative to Canada's national anthem, when CBC Radio legend Peter Gzowski ran The Great Canadian Song contest on his program *Morningside*, asking listeners for nominations and votes in 1995.

Stan was also known for the sea shanty "Barrett's Privateers," covered very recently by the metal folk band Alestorm. Lots of us know the chorus and love to sing along, especially in a well-heated, invitingly lit pub with dark paneled walls, comfortable chairs, and an impressive bar, tended by a friendly, knowledgeable local who is happy to chat about his town and his province. This is even better on a February night when you've wandered in from a road that has three feet of crusty, salt-dirtied snow pounded into its base and piled up on its edges. Maybe you're wearing two sweaters, leggings under your jeans, ski socks, mitts, toque, and a Hudson's Bay scarf that you've had pulled up over your mouth during the short walk from the car to the door and which is now damp and yucky. Or you've left the scarf down, wrapped around your neck to keep your throat from freezing and your face from looking silly, and your cheeks are now bright red and your nose is running.

You order a Canadian beer, which is made like they mean it, and a plate of poutine. The room is warm and about as convivial a place as you've ever been in. The band tunes up, they launch into "Barrett's Privateers", and, by the third time through the chorus? You know the words, and you're singing along. This may happen in a Nova Scotia town but it may just as easily happen in Ontario, Manitoba, or anywhere else in Canada.

I met Stan Rogers before his tragic and untimely death in 1983 and programmed his music on CBC Radio often. A Canadian treasure.

They love music in Nova Scotia and are rightfully very proud of their musicians and artists. You can find a huge violin on the waterfront in Sydney, live music in pubs and restaurants everywhere from Halifax to Lunenburg to the Cabot Trail and back again, and numerous festivals celebrating traditional and other types of music.

In North Sydney, driving off the ferry on Day Three, we followed about a hundred motorcycles. The route across Newfoundland and Labrador is a magnet for them, one that's on the 'someday' list for many. Long-distance motorcycle riding is one of those things in the 'you'll have to explain it, I don't get it' category for me. Thousands of miles can be challenging enough, especially if the landscape boredom level is high. Add to that a ferocious rainstorm or unexpected winds, and I have to wonder, where's the fun in that? It's true, though, that the comfort quotient on motorbikes has been improved tremendously.

I'm told that the overall riding experience has been adjusted and made 'smart' with technology, as have so many other things in so many other aspects of life. I might have to rethink things and give it a try.

You don't see the numerous signs reading "Bikers Welcome" in Canada that you see all over the back roads of the U.S., particularly in the warm, tourist towns of Florida and California. I'd heard that in some places there were complaints from the local residents about the numbers of motorcycle riders who'd already found their way to the area.

The ferry arrived about 6:00 p.m., and I suppose we could have pushed on, heading north toward Cape Breton Island, the Lakes, and the Cabot Trail, but I wanted to see those places in daylight, so we stayed that night in a small roadside place in Nova Scotia.

The Cabot Trail is named for Venetian explorer John Cabot, who had a commission from King Henry VII of England and arrived on the North American mainland in 1497, believing he had reached Asia. Some think he landed on Cape Breton and some at Cape Bonavista in Newfoundland. You pronounce his last name briskly, with a solid 't'. It's Kaa-but, not Kaa-boe, as I thought for a long time, while I still thought him to be from France, like Cartier and Champlain.

It was long past dark when we parked at the motel. The accommodations so far had covered a small range of options, with a few things standard and mandatory. A solid roof, not a tent. A bathroom no more than ten feet away. Washing facilities. Cooking facilities optional, a good restaurant preferred. This one, the first of three planned for Nova Scotia, was just a motel, with many motorcycles parked outside. Compared to the digs in St. John's and Corner Brook, it was a reminder of more basic accommodation. The television was built in about 1995, and the bathroom plumbing was equally ancient. The air conditioning was a rusted unit wedged into the window, which then made it impossible to close the curtains.

Food would probably make this all seem a little better. The meal in the restaurant was hearty and delivered with a smile. By the time I finished my fish and chips, I wasn't cranky anymore and I was ready to see the humor in the privacy and air-cooling challenges of the old motel.

It was a clear night, and the dark sky with its thousands of pinpoint stars looked amazing. Back in the motel room, I stared at the window and considered the problem. If you pulled the curtain across the window, you could get no air from the box into the room; if you didn't, you had the other guests walking by the window, able to look in at the bed, my badly packed suitcase and my stack of books. Not good and absolutely ripe for a rant about crappy rooms, overpriced motel chains, and isolation.

But there was a solution and it was easy. Drape the curtain around and over the AC box. Use hair clips to deal with any coverage gaps. Have a glass of wine. Go to sleep.

The next morning, we stopped at the A&W to get a coffee. The clerk was just opening up and was swatting the hundreds of mosquitoes that had somehow entered overnight. She mentioned that the Tim Horton's down the road was open twenty-four hours a day. Is that the way it is everywhere?

Apparently so. Tims (or Timmy's) is Canada's largest quick-service restaurant chain, and probably the oldest. It was founded with a single store in 1964 in Hamilton, Ontario and one of the co-founders was hockey legend Tim Horton. Starting with coffee and donuts, priced affordably (the first donuts, according to their website, cost ten cents) and currently much lower than some of its competitors, Tims has become a Canadian institution. The famous Canadian phrase "Double Double" (double cream, double sugar) originated here. In 1974, Tim Horton passed away, but the company continued and has grown into a large corporation, traded on the stock market and merged with others. "Always open" is their slogan.

Our destination today was Dundee Resort and Golf Club, in the Bras d'Or region of Nova Scotia. Bras d'Or — Arms of Gold—is sometimes referred to in the plural and sometimes in the singular. The area's claim to fame is an inland saltwater lake with spectacular scenery. We found lots of things to do here, and it was a perfect spot to choose as a launching point for a trip around the Cabot Trail on the coast roads of Cape Breton Island.

We found a lot of Scottish influence and history in Nova Scotia. If you look up 'Dundee', the first reference will be to Scotland's fourth-largest city. The number of other places named 'Dundee' is testament to the energy and curiosity of Scottish emigrants throughout the world.

My plans unfolded in an unpredictable blend of strict and flexible. I chose this resort on only two days' notice, after figuring out that the ferry option to and from Newfoundland was going to work, despite not having taken six months to plan it. When I called to book a hotel room, I was grateful not to get any attitude from the staffer who took my call. Maybe for some, it's an essentially boring job, and the only entertainment they have is to telegraph their disapproval or shock to the naïve traveler who had the audacity to try to book something on short notice. But, really, just tell me if you have room and if you can get us in or not.

Fortunately, Dundee Resort and Golf Club could and did, but I also had the feeling that the person I spoke with on the phone didn't feel the need to play any games or pretend that she was doing me a huge favor.

Her directions to get to the place were also delightful.

"You come across the causeway, stay right, go straight, go straight, till you get to the last set of lights," she said. "You can't go further, only left or right. Go left, then straight, straight and to old Number 4, past the superstore, just keep going straight."

It's a bit of an exaggeration to use the word 'resort' here if your expectation is based on one of those large establishments that run like a well-oiled machine in a place like Florida or Hawaii. Dundee Resort and Golf Club was quaint and quiet, the furniture was old, and the building a bit odd. That's a completely subjective observation, of course, and I was, as one of the masters of travel writing, Paul Theroux, writes in *Deep South*, "conscious that my journeys were as much about my life as about the places I was experiencing." But they did have a golf course, for those (not me) who play, and an amazing view of a lake, with the water a shade of cobalt blue. I saw many families here, a lot of them appearing to be in the midst of multigenerational reunions. The restaurant had a commanding view of the lake, with windows on three sides, and a menu that featured enough variation of Atlantic seafood to please any connoisseur.

The drive to get there was exciting and would be especially appealing for those of you sick of large highways with gas station chain stores every ten miles. A twisty road, lots of changes in elevation, and very few other vehicles—what more could you ask? The Zig was in eight-cylinder heaven.

I had chosen my playlists and CDs for this road trip very carefully. The complete program of one hundred songs is up on Spotify and is listed at the end of this book. I picked about ten songs for each province and bookended it with my four all-time favorite Canadian songs. It runs province by province, east to west, and you can listen to it that way or put it on shuffle and play 'Guess Which Province.'

It's called Canada150.RumbleStripBooks.DJG and you can hear it by searching Spotify.

Of course, they had to be Canadian songs, written and performed by Canadian artists. I wasn't a total stickler about it though; I did include covers of some tunes, if the cover version was an improvement or at least an interesting variation. Another allowable deviation was a standard or a classic whose composer or originator was less important than the stature of the song. What does that even mean, you ask?

An example is Ian and Sylvia's version of "Farewell to Nova Scotia." We don't know who wrote it and, for all we know, it could be a random German or Spaniard or Viking who happened to spend some time, fall in love with the place, and leave behind a folk song. That wouldn't then fit my criteria, strictly speaking, as a Canadian song, written by a Canadian, would it? It's been covered by artists from Ireland to Louisiana. But it's a song about a Canadian place and so it qualified.

So, songs about Canada and Canadian places, and songs by Canadian artists: The Guess Who, Michael Bublé, Johnny Reid, Joni Mitchell, Ian Tyson, Jesse Winchester, Lighthouse, Celine Dion, Neil Young, Bryan Adams, Leonard Cohen, Drake, k.d. lang, Great Big Sea, Diana

Krall, Bruce Cockburn, Robbie Robertson, Tom Cochrane, Chad Kroeger, Buffy Sainte-Marie, Amanda Marshall, and Oscar Peterson.

Here in Nova Scotia, we listened to Stan Rogers, Rita MacNeil, the Rankin family, and Ashley MacIsaac. From time to time, I shut off the CD player and the MP3 player to listen to the silence of the land I was moving through. At other times, I pulled out the smartphone and looked up the answers to questions that had occurred to me along the way. (I quickly learned in Canada to do this only occasionally. The data usage charges were extreme.) I did learn some quirky things, though: Did you know that Wilf Carter—aka Montana Slim, aka the Yodeling Cowboy, and one of the most popular singers on Tommy Hunter's TV show back in the day—was from Nova Scotia?

For those of you who are far too young to remember the Tommy Hunter Show—it was a Friday night tradition in many families to gather around the TV set to watch his country music program in the years from 1965 to 1992. Since then, Shania Twain, Johnny Reid, Aaron Pritchett, Terri Clark, and Paul Brandt are just a few of the names to add to the 'Canadian country singers' list.

Canadian musicians have survived and have carried their songs to all corners of the globe, thanks to a very important policy decision made by politicians in the sixties. Realizing that something had to be done to prevent the failure of Canadian creativity and popularity in the face of the competition and the sheer numbers of releases of records from the United States and from England, the Canadian government began to require that Canadian broadcasting and cable stations program 25 percent of their air time with content that was at least partly written, performed, presented, or produced by a Canadian. (As the years went by, the percentage was raised to 30 then 35 and, for some licenses, 40 percent.) These are summary numbers; there were exceptions and variations, based on geographic location, genre of music, time of day for the broadcast, etc. but the policy spanned the years from 1971 until 2012. These 'CanCon' rules meant that when I turned on my radio, as a teenager growing up in the Toronto area in the seventies, I heard Gordon Lightfoot, The Guess

Who, Rush, and Joni Mitchell, in addition to the Beatles, the Rolling Stones, Olivia Newton John, and Tina Turner, and that, today, I have a playlist of Canadian recording artists that is vibrant, lengthy, and multifaceted.

This is not a fact, by the way. Well, the vibrant, lengthy, multifaceted playlist is, but the impact of the CanCon rules is contentious. Many artists would say they would have made it anyway, and didn't need policy support; perhaps some of those who moved to the States and were discovered there would argue that talent rises and is undeniable. We also have those who argue that protectionism is always a bad thing, even cultural protectionism. That perspective has gained sway over the past five years and the policy has changed.

Pick your own point of view— I happen to think anybody who believes in the notion of a handicap in golf or a head start in any competitive environment would see the value in putting a fence around a garden and allowing it to grow, uninterrupted.

(Mixing too many metaphors, I know.)

If you disagree with my thoughts on supporting the arts and culture, write your own book.

Over dinner at Dundee Resort and Golf Club that night, Zig and I discussed the next day's drive but were soon (and easily) distracted by watching the cute two-year-olds making the room their own. In the morning, we got ready to drive the Cabot Trail. The Zig was pumped; he'd seen this road as a kid on one of those family trips featuring a tent trailer and many homemade sandwiches, and he was eager to see what might be familiar. Nova Scotia is renowned all over the world for this drive, and we'd been looking forward to it as a highlight of the trip. From the map, it looked as though driving clockwise should be the plan, but as we stood at the hotel desk talking to one of the staffers in the morning, Debra advised a shortcut to the town of Baddeck, then driving counterclockwise.

"You'll see more," she said. "If you're going counterclockwise, you'll be closer to the cliffs and the view."

Oh, good. And closer to the edge.

Baddeck is a charming town, the summer home of Alexander Graham Bell, the inventor of the telephone and the founder of AT&T. When we drove through, I saw the banners still up for the Baddeck Festival, just past. Next time. I think, on a future trip to Baddeck, I would plan more time for lunch or dinner, a few hours of shopping on the town's main street, and maybe a long walk rather than a drive though.

The main thing I noticed once we were headed north and were officially on the Cabot Trail was the condition of some of the guard rails, battered and bent from vehicles that had crashed into them. I could see paint scrapes on them, and I couldn't help but wonder about the outcomes of these encounters. I guess I can deduce, though, that if the guard rail was still there, even if dented, it had done its job.

We saw (and stopped for) a lot of construction work, particularly in the national park section of the trail, and I have to confess that, even with a determination to be positive, we found ourselves with the question, repeated in almost every province—couldn't, or shouldn't, they have done this before the summer of 2017, the big anniversary year? I'm sure there's probably a province-by-province explanation of highway costs, weather issues, and political influences that had a bearing on the answers to that question, but as the touring outsider, just passing through, I wasn't really interested. I just wanted to vent about sitting in this ... line of vehicles, one more time, waiting for the signal that we could get going again.

After an exciting few hours, alternating between breathtaking scenery with ocean views framed by battered guard rails and lengthy examinations of the back end of the car parked in front of us at the roadwork halt, we pulled in at Ingonish Beach. This is one of the gems of the Cabot Trail—a beautiful beach of pebbles and stones, then a strip of sand roping the bright blue sea. Many people had staked out their space with beach blankets and chairs and were plunging into the water for a swim. It looked far too cold for me.

It's always fun, at these historic scenic sites, to imagine what the ancient explorers thought, as they arrived at this place for the first time—whether they were explorers from across the Atlantic in Spain, France, or Greenland, or questers from just a few dozen miles away. Did they have the same sense of 'just passing through?' Was it a location with a history of joy felt here or of dread? Did they stand on the shore and look outward over the ocean, contemplating what might lie on the land on the other side?

As it turned out, we didn't go the full circuit around the Trail that day. Every day of this journey had a tentative plan for distance to be covered and stopping points, and the calculation for the Cabot Trail had not included so much construction. Driving through the national park we were stopped a total of about two hours, at several roadwork spots. I lost track of how much more time was spent navigating single-lane traffic through other areas. I had set aside a week for the Maritimes and Newfoundland and Labrador. Adding an additional day for doing the full circuit of the Cabot Trail would throw that plan off. I figured I'd seen enough to pick up what I wanted to see of Cape Breton, and I was anxious for a look at Halifax before I said farewell to Nova Scotia. So we drove to the northernmost point of the trail and then turned around in our tracks and headed back.

I hate this, by the way. I hate going over ground I've already covered, retracing steps, backing up, repeating, duplicating, whatever they call it. I don't mean metaphorically, or in life, or while practicing a piece of music—just in geography. If I am even 30 percent of the way around a circle, I'd rather continue going forward, rather than return to the beginning. But sometimes you just have to give in gracefully. It made more sense to turn back than to go forward, not knowing how much more construction delay there might be yet to come and not knowing whether the views on the west side of the island were worth the extra time. I suppose I could have canvassed the opinions of a few dozen fellow travelers who had taken the time to post here or there online, but I could have ended up spending as much time reading screens (at the jaw-dropping Canadian cell data rates) as I would have sitting in construction line-ups.

Next time I visit Nova Scotia, I'll cover the second half of the Cabot Trail, but this time, it was time to move on to Halifax. This is a legendary city to me, especially because of lines of lyrics from two songs that bubble up to the surface of my mind: "Barrett's Privateers" and "Dancing in the Street" (The Mamas & the Papas' version).

Halifax, the capital of Nova Scotia, sits on a harbor that it shares with Dartmouth. Harbor is one of those words that seems misspelled to Canadians. Even though, for the purposes of this book, the publisher is using the standard American spellings, place names and proper names that include a word that Canadians spell with a 'u' will get one. Therefore, Halifax Harbour. (Zig wants to know whether Dartmouth is, or was ever, Dartmoth. Gotta love a funny man.)

For this stop, we were staying at a downtown hotel located right on the waterfront, next to the historic district, and featuring doormen wearing kilts. The weather in Halifax was rainy, and we saw the historic district and the waterfront through a mist. When we pulled up to the hotel front door, the young man who helped with our bags couldn't wait to talk about road trips.

"You're a long way from home," he commented, pointing at our Georgia license plate.

"You bet. We're on a cross-Canada tour to celebrate the 150th birthday," Zig confirmed.

"I've done that drive," the doorman said. "Not exactly that drive, I mean, not the U.S. part. But I drove from here to Jasper last year. With my girlfriend. She likes road trips."

"You have to like road trips if you're going to drive from Halifax to Jasper," I agreed.

"Next time I'll go right across to Vancouver, then go south to California," he decided. And another dream was born.

While we were in Halifax, Zig took advantage of the opportunity to see the last of the corvettes. It's a ship, not a car—although the cars were named after these vessels in the fifties. This one is on display on the waterfront next to the Maritime Museum of the Atlantic, one of one hundred and twenty-three built in shipyards in Québec, the

Maritimes, Ontario, and British Columbia. They were deployed by the Canadian Navy in World War II, escorting convoys of supply ships and oil tankers across the Atlantic and the Zig's father served on one. All of the corvettes are gone now, but this one was found being used as a research vessel and was restored as a Naval Memorial and a National Historic Site. You can tour the HMCS Sackville and see the conditions in which the sailors lived and worked.

It was a brief sampling of Halifax and left me wanting to return to see more. Our next stop was to be Peggy's Cove, south of Halifax. The weather conditions were still wet when we left, and we couldn't see much of the ocean as we drove along the coast. I quickly drew the conclusion that here was another reason that a return visit would be necessary.

Peggy's Cove is a very small rural community on the east side of St. Margaret's Bay (and I had to wonder whether the saint was the 'Peggy' who was referred to). It's famous for Peggy's Point Lighthouse, established in 1868, and has become a tourist magnet. Later that night, I looked up a few more details. Apparently many people believe that 'Peggy' was the sole survivor of a nearby shipwreck who stayed on and made her home in the village.

I also discovered online that there is a resort in Thailand that has taken Peggy's Cove as its inspiration, with a restaurant called Lighthouse and buildings that look like replicas of the fishing village houses we saw in the Nova Scotia Peggy's Cove. It's a small world.

Time to say farewell to Nova Scotia and turn toward Canada's smallest province, where the power of the written word has created a magnet far beyond what might be expected from sheer scenic beauty.

Some famous people born in, educated in, housed or claimed by Nova Scotia?
Hockey player Sidney Crosby. Singer Anne Murray. Actress Ruby Keeler. Artist Alex Colville. Singer Sarah McLachlan. Psychologist Donald O. Hebb. Inventor

Alexander Graham Bell.

What to see next time?
Lunenburg. This town on the east coast, south of Peggy's Cove, was just a bit too far for us to go on this trip, but it's top of the list for a return visit to the province.

Louisburg. This historic fort, east of Sydney, was founded by the French in 1713. If you go at the right time of year (mid-May to mid-October), you'll see museum guides dressed in period clothes, tour two-and-a-half kilometers of walls thirty feet high (and in some places thirty-six feet thick) and, a short distance away, you'll see Canada's first lighthouse, built in 1734.

What to see more of?
Baddeck. There was something about the appearance and the vibe in this little place that made it stand out, even in thirty short minutes of 'just passing through'. Plus, it's fun to say.

Halifax. The preservation of the city's historic waterfront has been celebrated in many places far more substantial than this book, but let me add my voice to the chorus: we would all be the poorer for it if so many people had not combined efforts to care for this city's roots.

What to see less of?
The cliffside curves on the Cabot Trail. It's perhaps the wrong confession to make if you are a travel writer who includes road trips as part of her repertoire, but I don't enjoy narrow roads with tight turns. I'm not saying I would cross off the Cabot Trail from my list of places to go in Nova Scotia, but I would be prepared, and maybe take a chill pill or two. Make sure somebody else is driving. Don't be surprised by the gouges and dents in the metal guard rails along the road. Keep eyes closed, if safe.

Surprises?
The Cajun culture in Nova Scotia, sustained by the descendants of the Acadians, the same people who were

among the settlers of Louisiana.

African-Canadian culture, reflective of the slaves who escaped before and during the U.S. Civil War in the 19th century.

The lack of moose. I drove for nearly three weeks across Canada and saw a moose only once, at a great distance and only for a couple of seconds. That was not in Nova Scotia.

Chapter Three

PRINCE EDWARD ISLAND

Anne with an E

I'll save you the moose suspense, if there is any. Didn't see one in Prince Edward Island either.
 But I did see a blue jay (the provincial bird) and cows (both the living kind and the fake one outside the Cows ice cream and cheese factory).
 I also saw a farm that was the inspiration for one of the most popular novels of all time.
 Prince Edward Island is a small island (5,660 square kilometers) with rolling green hills, fertile fields, charming farmhouses, and sparkling white churches. We drove onto the island via the Confederation Bridge, a relatively recent addition to the travel options to P.E.I. We'd arrived at the mainland end of the bridge by way of New Brunswick, but for purposes of this book I'm going to leave all the New Brunswick sights to the next chapter, to look at all at once, rather than drop Prince Edward Island into the middle of it, like a dessert in the middle of a five-course meal.
 We drove up twisty back roads that climbed to lookouts commanding views of endless blue ocean and distant shores. Sandy beaches hug the coasts near beautiful small towns. You cover 224 kilometers going lengthwise, and from six to sixty-four kilometers crossing the width. If you're on a bicycle, it can be a bit longer, with 273 kilometers quoted as the length of the island, tip to tip. It is the smallest province in Canada, both in land and

population (about 146,000 people). It is known for potatoes, sandy beaches, red soil, and Green Gables.

Yes, the upper case 'g' is supposed to be there. In both cases. More on that to come, later.

The province's current name was adopted in 1799 in honor of Prince Edward, the fourth son of King George III and father of Queen Victoria. Prior to that, it was named St. John's Island after the Treaty of Paris, a post-war negotiation in which it was ceded to the British by the French. French traveler Jacques Cartier had explored it in the sixteenth century and named it Ile Saint-Jean, and the original settlers were the Acadians, relatives of the Cajuns who brought the French flavor to the bayous of the southern U.S. Originally it was called Abegweit or Epekwitk, the name given the island by the Mi'kmaq who were living there when the French voyageurs arrived.

The source for all this, by the way, was Wikipedia, which is, as I've mentioned, a compilation of all of the information and all of the knowledge of all of the people in the world who care to pick up a computer, log in, and add to it. (Citation needed.) Seriously, I am deeply ambivalent about Wikipedia and have been for years, but I can't deny the convenience of the thing. The overall accuracy seems to be robust enough too. Every once in a while, I look up something obscure, just to see whether they have it right, and I haven't landed on a whopper of a mistake yet. But I did want to point out to you again that, although this book has some stats and some proper nouns in it, it isn't intended to be a textbook or even a journalistic book. It is intended as a collection of personal observations and reactions. Please don't use it as a source for your essay, your presentation, your comments to your boss, or anything else you might be graded on.

P.E.I. is referred to as the "birthplace of Confederation" because of a conference that took place in Charlottetown in 1864 that led, eventually, to the creation of Canada in 1867. Prince Edward Island joined Canada in 1873. Yes, there is a discrepancy in the years there. Like any historical account, it's complicated, and I don't want to digress from the primary purpose and tone of this book which is to cross Canada in honor of its 150th birthday in an indigo convertible, with a light heart all the way. But, essentially, P.E.I. was there at the start of the conversation, took a break, and then returned later on. In 1867, the Dominion of Canada was made up of Nova Scotia, New Brunswick, Québec, and Ontario.

In 1870, Manitoba and the Northwest Territories joined Confederation. British Columbia saddled up in 1871, P.E.I. in 1873, Yukon in 1898, Saskatchewan and Alberta in 1905, and Newfoundland in 1949. Nunavut was created from what was previously part of the Northwest Territories in 1999, and Newfoundland and Labrador was drawn as a province in 2001.

Does this mean more cross-country drives to honor other 150th anniversaries—in 2020, in 2021, in 2023, in 2048, in 2055, and in 2099? Sure, why not? It's like considering any reason for a party or an event: any excuse is a good excuse.

Prince Edward Island is not only the birthplace of Confederation. It's also the birthplace of many notable Canadians, including a significant number of hockey players and poets. It is probably most famous, though, as the homeland of a fictional character beloved all over the world—Anne of Green Gables.

Anne is the island's main claim to fame and its major export over the past one hundred years plus. *Anne of Green Gables* was written by Canadian author Lucy Maud Montgomery and published in 1908. I was a girl when I became acquainted with Anne, after my grandmother gave me the book.

Anne is a child who comes to live on a farm called Green Gables with brother and sister Matthew and Marilla Cuthbert. After they decided to provide a home to an orphan in return for help on their farm, eleven-year-old Anne Shirley is sent in place of the sturdy teenage boy Matthew and Marilla expected. Anne charms her way into their hearts and into a series that carried her through her childhood years up to age twenty-five, in later books *Anne of Avonlea*, *Anne of the Island*, and *Anne of Windy Poplars*. Her story has been translated into thirty different languages and has sold more than fifty million copies. I introduced my daughters to her in their early reading days. Over the years, I met many other Canadian women who had fond memories of Anne and her adventures, and one or two who said their mothers had named them for her. The book became a play and a musical, it has been turned into (half a dozen) television series in Canada, and it is also a perennial bestseller in Japan. Tens of thousands of tourists come every year to see the P.E.I. farmhouse that was the model for the setting of Lucy Maud Montgomery's novel.

And I was one of them. A visit to Green Gables was high on my list, not just for this first-time trip to Prince Edward Island and to the Maritime provinces, but also because it is Canada's 150th birthday and there are just a few things that ya gotta do.

Almost every Anne book I've ever seen and every TV show or movie depiction shows Anne as a freckled girl with long red hair in braids. It's interesting to see in an image of the first edition that there is no straw hat or pair of red braids in sight. The Anne on that cover looks like an elegant, turn-of-the-century young lady with wavy hair coiled against her neck; in fact, there's a rather interesting account of Lucy Maud Montgomery keeping a photograph of Evelyn Nesbit up on her wall as inspiration for Anne while she was writing. Evelyn Nesbit was a very successful model and actress of that time who later went on to notoriety as the wife of Harry Kendall Thaw, the killer of architect Stanford White.

You have to wonder if it's true, though, since chapter two of the book describes Anne with red hair, in braids. (Recent illustrations of Anne with blonde hair generated a negative flurry in Comment World.) That's the thing about Wikipedia information—it might be true and it might not be. As with any time you're told something—consider the source. If you doubt Wikipedia too much, though, you're dissing all the accurate, carefully researched, and kindly provided pieces, but if you take it as word-for-word reality, you're being too trusting, perhaps, and you're bound to bump into mistakes. The question is whether you'll run into more mistakes than you would anywhere else.

Until the early nineties, the only way to get to P.E.I.

was on a ferry, and weather conditions made winter travel unpredictable. Construction on the Confederation Bridge began in October 1993 and finished in 1997, and, during the eighties, before a public vote gave the government the go-ahead, controversy raged over whether to provide this sort of year-round, easy access to P.E.I.. Today, this bridge connecting the island to the province of New Brunswick and to the rest of Canada, sees four thousand crossings a day. It is eight miles long and is one of the engineering feats of the twentieth century.

The toll is $47.73 CAD currently, a discovery that may shock many American drivers who are used to approaching a toll plaza where they want one or two dollars. Even in New York City and New Jersey these days, the highest they'll charge is about eighteen dollars. Before we arrived, I checked on the fee with the Confederation Bridge website (alright, I do range beyond Wikipedia) and discovered they also charge another $40 for "Apprehensive Drivers". This made me laugh. Meaning what? Someone who has a phobia about bridges? About this one in particular? About Confederation, maybe—somehow who had watched too much CBC Television coverage of election results and Québec separation referendum ballots over the years? Do you self-identify as Apprehensive? How do they know?

But after we drove on with no tollbooths anywhere to be seen, I realized that the toll gets paid when you are leaving. By then they know whether you stopped halfway across the bridge, slowed down to ten kilometers per hour, making all the other drivers crazy, or required one of their staff to drive you back across the bridge.

Neither the Zig nor I have any issues with crossing bridges or with islands, and we managed to keep that portion of the trip budget under control. You can't see much as you go across, and I was looking forward to reaching the other side for that reason. We decided to look in on Charlottetown on the way back and headed straight for Green Gables. It is near Cavendish, on the north side of the island, a lovely cruise through rolling hills, past fertile farm fields, and through charming little towns. We stopped for lunch and were offered a menu that contained an overwhelming number of fresh seafood choices.

Green Gables was a busy place, with a well-tended parking lot in a location that was easy to find. Clearly, they are used to attracting the attention of thousands of tourists. I thought it was an attraction that was positioned nicely, somewhere in the middle between mega theme park and honkytonk lame excuse for a museum. You leave your vehicle and walk along a short path to the farmyard, the barn, the garden, and a couple of other outbuildings. The house itself isn't festooned with gables, but what was there was green. They have a ramp built to allow for wheelchair, walker, or just stair-averse access to the house, although once inside, if you want to see the upper floor you'll need to be easy with stairs. The place was packed, and we shuffled along in a line, peering at the old-fashioned furniture, tools, and clothing.

I think if you weren't a fan of the books you'd have a difficult time figuring out what you were doing there. But fans of Anne and of the books would be beaming ... and I saw quite a few of them there. There was a steady stream of visitors waiting their turns to have their photo taken by the front door and a long line winding its way through the barn.

At regular intervals, an actress playing Anne came out into the farmyard and the visitors flocked to have their photos taken with her. In the gift shop attached to the farm, straw hats with long red braids attached are one of the featured items for sale, and in the hour I was there I saw half a dozen girls wearing them. Not a fashion choice for me, but I did load up on Anne of Green Gables tea, soap, coffee mug, bookmark, and a copy of *Anne of Avonlea*.

With a red-haired Anne on the cover.

Why have the Anne books become classics? We could probably discuss the vivid characters, the (at that time) remote setting, the unique stories, the universality of the themes, but I think it may be that it all comes down to language. As one of the leading lights in travel memoir, Jack Kerouac, wrote in The Dharma Bums, "One day I will find the right words, and they will be simple." Lucy Maud put this book into the world using simple words—the

right words—and Anne of Green Gables will never disappear.
   The visit to the inspiration for the setting didn't disappoint. It lived up to my expectations, not because the farmhouse was particularly pretty nor the landscape exactly as described in the book. It was because with every step and every glimpse of something in the house, the barn, the garden, or the surrounding places, I was reminded of a scene I'd loved in the book or an experience in my own life that I'd had while reading the book.
   I think a book is a lot like a scent or a line from a song. When you smell or hear it, having been in an emotional moment when you first experienced it, it takes you back. People sometimes refer to 'the soundtrack of your life', and I think there is a bookshelf of your life too.
   The visit to Green Gables lived up to my expectations because of what I brought to it, rather than what was actually there. You might or might not have the same result. I hope you do.
   All of this was obviously a tourism driver for P.E.I.; the people seemed to be very conscious and appreciative of it. The rest of the town hadn't really jumped on the Anne bandwagon, though. I didn't see Anne Mini Golf or Gilbert Bait & Tackle or Marilla's Down Home Cooking Diner. Thank goodness. Just gorgeous scenery and interesting roads to drive—more than enough 'added value'.
   Anne of Green Gables is probably the most successful Canadian novel ever published, but it is only one name to check if you want to talk about Canadian writers and stories (and P.E.I. is only one place to highlight). Alice Munro (born in Ontario and a long-time resident of British Columbia) won the Nobel Prize for Literature in 2013. Margaret Atwood (born in Ontario) gave the world *The Handmaid's Tale* and many other books. John McCrae (born in Ontario) wrote the poem "In Flanders Fields", Mordecai Richler (born in Québec) created the character Duddy Kravitz, and Leonard Cohen (also from Québec) composed the song "Hallelujah", covered by more than two hundred other singers, in addition to hundreds of poems, stories, novels, and songs.

That's barely a start, just scratching the surface.

Literary pilgrimages in Canada don't have to start and end with Green Gables, either. There is the Pierre Berton Writer's Retreat house in Dawson City, Yukon; Margaret Laurence House in Neepawa, Manitoba; Stephen Leacock Museum in Orillia, Ontario; McCrae House in Guelph, Ontario; Carol Shields Memorial Labyrinth in Winnipeg; and the Al Purdy statue in Toronto.

Our next stop after Green Gables was Charlottetown, the provincial capital. Renovation work of some kind was underway on the main civic building, the one that you see on the back of the paper money in Canada, and plywood covered the windows. It was not the only architectural or scenic game in town, however, and the tree-lined streets were another tourist draw. Charlottetown was another spot in the Maritimes where I could imagine pitching my metaphorical tent for a week or more.

Later that evening, I turned on my computer and started to look over the day's notes. Up to that moment, I had been keeping a few road notes on paper and dictating observations into my phone, when I didn't want to look away from the passing landscape. I had downloaded a mobile app that let me dictate words that magically appeared on the screen as a document that my computer could process. Then I could email it to myself later and play with it all I wanted on a screen that didn't require a magnifying glass to read and a keyboard that didn't require incessant correction of the characters I typed in because my fingertips are normal sized and the smartphone keyboard is built for a person with toothpicks for fingers.

It took some practice to get used to the app and to the process of dictating. You had to say the pronunciation, periods, commas, and the like. You had to spell any weird words and, even then, they didn't come out right. I found that there are some words my phone seems to know and blast onto the screen in a micro-second and other (quite common) ones that seemed to perplex and even infuriate it.

It didn't take long before the app itself seemed to have a personality. Maybe I just awarded it one, in order to keep myself from becoming so annoyed with it that my blood pressure was at risk. I decided to name it after a famous TV secretary from a show back in the day when the word 'secretary' meant more than a piece of antique furniture. Miss Hathaway was the name of the character on *The Beverly Hillbillies* and it popped into my head completely uninvited; the memory is a fascinating thing.

At first when I spoke to Miss Hathaway, I felt incredibly self-conscious. But as the hours went by, I started to feel a bit like I imagined a stand-up comedian would feel. I was trying to keep the tone light and affectionate—funny, but not sarcastic, mean-spirited, or full of complaints. That would have been an easy road to take. There were many problems and challenges during a travel day; there are everywhere, of course. But I was determined to point out the creative solution, not the problems, over and over. Partly, I thought that all that stress on stress would get boring and, partly, I thought it would drag me down so much I might not finish the project.

I had a fantasy that writing this book would be an easy matter of chatting away to a friendly piece of technology while I sped along through the Canadian landscape, past emerald green lakes, fields of golden wheat, exciting cities, and the occasional moose.

It turned out that my fantasy was unrealistic. The words that Miss Hathaway delivered were so fractured that major surgery had to be done to make them even remotely comprehensible.

Just for fun, here's an example of what she delivered after processing my spoken words about Prince Edward Island:

So prince Edward Island is small and we get to it by way of an 8 mile bridge that was built after much controversy and beat out of her how to arrange a crossing up till that point there was a ferry . . . The houses are starting along this road to look like pictures without one there is exactly the shape of Green Gables BLI as famous as the location for a novel called Annagreen Gables just one of my favorites when I was a kid . . . Prince Edward Island is known for speeches and we're going to check out some of the

white sand beach is here there and what else they have going on . . .
Everything looks really healthy right greens bright yellows bright goals. The GPS has us on a route to the cabin dish. Research needed on Lucy mod Montgomery I do know that she went by the initials only. . . I just finished looking at Green Gables and now we're driving Highway 13 heading toward Charlotte town of its farm country will be at the top down on the convertible and so we're getting a fool measure of coarse country yeah I think it is horses or ferdle. Eye. Zer.
First red those books when I was about seven or eight years old and might navigate me a copy and it was just a cake to see all the places that are mentioned in the book . . .

My favorite part was the "fool measure of coarse country". Almost poetic, that. I also loved the way App Miss Hathaway translated my "it was just a slice" (a cliché I confess to using frequently) to "it was just a cake".

What else is Prince Edward Island famous for? Potatoes (the province grows a third of Canada's potatoes), beaches (ninety), golf courses (thirty-three), and food (lobster, oysters, mussels—and potatoes).

It is also the home of the longest running musical ever (no, not Wikipedia— Guinness World Records, 2014): Anne of Green Gables the Musical (of course). It was produced in 1965 at the Charlottetown Festival for the first time and has been presented annually ever since.

Lucy Maud, Don Harron, and all the others expressed their love for P.E.I. through the English language. Next I was about to roll into the province where they express their love for their island in two official languages.

Famous people born in, educated in, housed or claimed by Prince Edward Island?
Poet Milton Acorn. Actor Jonathan Torrens. Writer Lucy Maud Montgomery. Actress Claire Rankin. Golfer Lorie Kane. Olympic bobsledder David MacEachern.

What to see next time?
A play. Live theater is another thing that Prince Edward

Island is famous for. The Charlottetown Festival, Mi'kmaq Legends, Anne and Gilbert at The Guild, half a dozen other theaters in active production every year.

What to see more of?
The P.E.I. beaches. My time was limited, that's my excuse. With only one day to get an overall sense of the place and to see something as legendary as Green Gables, I had to make a choice. Several choices in fact, and I skipped Cavendish Beach, even though I was very nearby.

I also skipped doing a careful, leisurely investigation of Charlottetown. I would add "Prince Edward Island urban life" as another thing to see more of.

What to see less of?
Roadwork, construction scaffoldings, and boarded up windows on heritage buildings being restored. Can't this be done at some time other than the summer holidays, prime tourist, and traveler visiting time? Can't it be done faster?

Surprises?
How beautiful it is.

The huge crowds at Green Gables, with license plates from Missouri, California, Oregon, Tennessee. I thought I would be special, with mine from Georgia, come all the way to Prince Edward Island, but I got not a blink, never mind a double-take or a "wow, you've come a long way." I guess they're used to it.

Chapter Four

NEW BRUNSWICK

A river runs backwards through it

Thanks to the strength of the tides in the Bay of Fundy, the waters of the Saint John River actually run upstream twice a day. I'd heard that before—it's one of those facts that they tell western Canadian school children about remarkable things going on in other parts of their country.

But the two languages policy in New Brunswick was one thing I hadn't heard much about or remembered. New Brunswick is the only Canadian province that is officially bilingual. Hah! Didn't know that, did you? Neither did I, and I lived in Canada for many years.

If I were in a trivia contest and that was the question—"Which Canadian province is officially bilingual?"—I would lose the points. I thought it was Québec, I am embarrassed to admit. I am checking lots of facts as I go (for my own curiosity but also to be helpful to you, if you are a foreigner traveling across Canada, or a Canadian with as many assumptions and misconceptions as I have), and it turns out that the official language of Québec is French. Canada is officially bilingual (two official languages, French and English), and most of the provinces are officially English (except for New Brunswick. And Manitoba, technically, as it offers bilingualism in all legal matters).

Right now, I am stuck on how informative to become

here. Are you bored? I could go into a lot of detail and a truckload of subtle points, political points, historical points, and complicated economics, but if I include too many, you'll feel like you are in textbook land and I don't want that. It's a vacation, right?

Or as we say in Canada, a holiday, eh?

The root of the word 'vacation' and the reason it is used more commonly in the U.S. is an interesting story. (And that is root in both countries, by the way.) Back at the turn of the twentieth century, wealthy folks in New York, Boston, Philadelphia, and Washington, D.C. would head north in the summer to what they called 'camps' for a break from the city heat. They referred to "vacating" their primary residences. Vacate, vacation.

Some of the people from New York, Boston, Philadelphia, or Washington, D.C. went a long way north. The Roosevelts, Franklin D. and Eleanor, had a summer place on Campobello Island, New Brunswick, for example.

I saw New Brunswick in a two-part visit, the first on the way into Canada and heading for our starting point in Newfoundland, and then on the way north and west toward Québec.

New Brunswick was one of the four original provinces at Confederation in 1867. I could argue that there were actually three, since Québec and Ontario were conjoined in the Province of Canada until the actual moment of Confederation, when they became the two separate ones. But it was indisputable that the other two were Nova Scotia and New Brunswick, no dividing or splitting involved there.

Sometimes, when you read a history of Canada, it seems impossible to avoid the conclusion that separating and uniting, drawing and redrawing the borders, is this country's favorite pastime, its defining characteristic. It makes me think of grade school science class, looking at an amoeba on a slide, growing and shrinking, sending shoots of itself off in one direction or another, morphing and changing and shape-shifting. But maybe that's just a description of national politics and boundaries everywhere.

You have to take the big picture to get that, though. Of

course, if you think of the past forty or fifty years, that isn't the case. Saskatchewan has sat there, solid and serious with those borders on its east and west sides, for what seems like forever. But pull back the focus, a hundred and twenty years even, to pre-1905 when it joined Canada, and where was the boundary then? There was none, at least none like the lines we have on a map today. There were territories that the native nations outlined, areas defined by seasonal migrations and traditional experiences. Before that, who knows?

Wherever the boundaries were, they are far, far beyond the scope of this account of a nineteen-day-trip across what became the Dominion of Canada in 1867. I will try to stay in focus.

When you drive into Canada from Maine, you have several choices of entry points. We drove in via St. Stephen, New Brunswick. On the American side, it is a little town called Calais. The plan was to drive the two-and-a-half hours to Moncton, New Brunswick's largest city, stay overnight, and then carry on to Newfoundland to find Mile Zero.

Maine is a beautiful state, filled with intriguing forests, lovely coves, and seaside towns, and no moose (that I saw, anyway). I definitely put it on the 'have to return here, and soon' list. I had expected the landscape between Maine, USA and New Brunswick, Canada to be essentially the same. Borders are sometimes logical and have been drawn to follow some feature, like the Savannah River dividing the states of Georgia and South Carolina, but sometimes they are just arbitrary and you have to drill down deeply into the region's history to find out why the line was drawn there. When you look at a map, you can't see any obvious reason for the border there, no change from mountain to valley or lakeshore to forest.

But the last few miles as you approach the border on the U.S. side are about as Maine as you can get: thick forest, narrow highway, jagged rocks, and towering trees.

I had not expected to find another Calais, so far from France, and yet here it was in the state of Maine, a little urban collection just to the west of St. Stephen, New Brunswick on the Canadian side.

Over dinner in Moncton after driving through the province's rolling hills, we agreed it was easy to see why people buy property in the Maritimes in summer—the provinces are incredibly beautiful. The smitten tourist buys in haste, perhaps, then repents at leisure during the winter blizzards. I saw a lot of signs that said 'watch out for falling snow and ice' on gas station roofs and supermarket overhangs, something difficult to visualize on this sunny August day. New Brunswick, I've heard though, is absolutely paradise if you love snow and winter sports. It has annual snowfall of 200 to 400 centimeters—that's about 80 to 155 inches! The snowmobile season is one of the longest south of the Arctic, they say.

Alex the server passed by our table frequently after we'd shared with him our plans for this anniversary road trip. He had nothing but enthusiasm—quite a contrast to the border services officer who, earlier that day, had seemed skeptical about my plans.

"How long will you be in Canada?" he asked.

"Three weeks," I said.

"And you're planning to get to Victoria in that time?" He shook his head. Why, because he thought I must not have looked at a map and therefore didn't have any idea how wide Canada really is? Because he suspected I wasn't really who I claimed to be and wasn't really a Canadian, if I thought Canada could be driven in three weeks?

Judgment everywhere. Maybe he doesn't do twelve-hour days in the car, but I do.

After you answer the questions and cross the border, you find yourself in a landscape that feels open and different. The reasons can be figured out pretty quickly. On the Canadian side, they've built the highway much wider, four lanes, with an expansive median, and have cut down the trees on either side.

The weather was glorious, a day for appreciating the brilliance of the engineer who thought of the drop top. What was it about convertibles that made them so appealing? Maybe it was just a return to the past, when we all rode around in carts or carriages.

Along the road, I saw small polite billboards, very different from the large American ones that shout at you, then tell you who won their state beauty queen contest, who could get you millions of dollars in a personal-injury lawsuit, and where to go to get the absolute best in local foodstuffs like peanuts, peaches, or lobster. Many of the Canadian ones were about half the size, not as colorful, and more preoccupied with giving you the facts than convincing you to buy. Generally, in Canada the language and words used tend to be more reserved, too—less forceful, less excited, and usually more direct. Manitoba's widest cellular network. Canadian Tire Store and Service Open 7 Days a Week.

This second leg of our New Brunswick visit began with a drive toward Fredericton, the province's capital. While there is lots of farmland to look at, there is also lots of muskeg. I also saw dozens more 'beware of moose' signs.

And—I saw a moose in New Brunswick! There, that's the end to the suspense. It was light brown in color, head down, off in the distance, among the trees. Just for a second, but still. I wondered again about the signs—with all the moose fencing, did they really ever get out anywhere near the highway? I guess it happened often enough that someone decided the signs were necessary, and so were the metal structures the trucks had mounted on their front grilles.

What else is New Brunswick known for? As mentioned in the earlier comments about vacations, it was the summer home of American President Franklin Delano Roosevelt. He and Eleanor visited every summer with their family, spending two months sailing, socializing, and reading, until the early twenties when he became ill and unable to walk more than very short distances. Today, government and academic conferences book into his former home, now part of the Roosevelt Campobello International Park. Members of the public can see it too.

What else? The Bay of Fundy has the highest tides in the world. Mount Allison University has the highest number of Rhodes scholars per capita of any educational institution in the Commonwealth.

And one of the world's largest lobsters is to be found at Shediac, New Brunswick. It's a sculpture thirty-five feet long, sixteen feet high, the whole thing weighing ninety tonnes (that's almost 200,000 pounds) and made of concrete and reinforced steel. Apparently, there is some dispute about the 'world's largest', with a statue in South Australia also claiming the title.

New Brunswick also has a Magnetic Hill, near Moncton, and this turned out to be one of the highlights of the trip, just in the 'delight' factor. It's an optical illusion in which you go backward up a hill in your vehicle. You go down the hill, put the car in neutral, and go upward, backwards, steering as you go. You pay six dollars for this experience.

While I was there, a busload of tourists arrived and stood alongside the road with cameras, watching me in my convertible and shooting video. Two women stared and pointed at the car's front wheels, and I wished I could see what they were seeing. (I've checked out the usual online site suspects but nothing has turned up yet.)

"Prepare to be amazed!" said the advertising, and I was—both prepared and amazed. I was happy we sought this out, since I'd heard about the Magnetic Hill in New Brunswick since I was a child. It was one of those jealousy-inducing places, when you heard classmates recount visits to it in their what-I-did-on-my-summer-vacation (or holiday) reports in September. They've added a mini golf course, a butterfly world, fast-food restaurants, and a casino to try to make the destination a little more worthwhile (but definitely more costly).

In New Brunswick, I also saw numerous red maple leaf flags and 'Happy Birthday, Canada' signs. Typically, Canadians aren't that demonstrably patriotic, especially compared to Americans, who put up and keep up a flag at almost every opportunity and on every special occasion. But there seemed to be a spirit of celebration all across the Atlantic provinces that summer, and the red maple leaf added to it. The maple leaf was made the core of the Canadian flag in 1965, but the symbolic significance of the emblem goes back to the nineteenth century, when politicians of the day referred to it in speeches, the song "The Maple Leaf Forever" became a second national anthem, and various groups began to adopt it as a mark.

Fredericton is a lovely small city and one of the jewels of Canada, if you ask me. Situated on the Saint John River, it has a layout and a streetscape that is so pleasing. The scale, the spatial relationships between buildings and open spaces, and the trees that line the streets all contribute. Fredericton is the provincial capital, and the stately legislative building sits just across the street from the Lord Beaverbrook Art Gallery. Nearby, a playhouse and a convention center offer services for arts and commerce. The river seems to be the focal point for the city's life. On a floating dock, many people strolled at sunset and one group of three young women did yoga poses in the setting sun.

I started chatting with some of the people working on a restaurant patio with a view near the river; one mentioned that "you never get tired of it" and they all vigorously agreed.

We also talked with a young father who had his family with him on vacation. When he heard about our 150 project, he said that driving cross-Canada was a dream of his too. The idea seemed to put sparks in the eyes of everybody we mentioned it to.

I think that's because most people recognize the difference between their imagination and reality. Samuel Johnson wrote that the "use of traveling is to regulate imagination with reality—instead of thinking of how things may be, see them as they are." It's when you get out on the open road that you are truly finding out how things really are, rather than imagining them or taking someone else's word for it.

We left Fredericton on a gorgeous morning the next day—64 degrees and not a cloud in the sky. Our plan was to drive 112 kilometers to Hartland, New Brunswick, home of The World's Longest Covered Bridge. It is 1,282 feet long and promoted as one of Canada's most romantic spots. For a while there, I was misspelling Hartland, adding an early 'e' because it seemed to make sense that one of the most romantic spots would have something to do with a 'heart-land'.

The bridge was first opened in 1901. It is just one lane. You wait at one end until it seems to be clear, put on your headlights and drive across. Slowly.

And, in our case, twice. We wanted to retrace our steps (wheel rotations, actually) and get north and heading west through the next province, Québec. North of Hartland, you are heading for Rivière du Loup, as you hug the border with Maine. We've covered 6,400 kilometers so far, by driving back, forth, and around in a relatively small area, the Atlantic provinces. We were about to turn left to go west and cover a much wider expanse.

This is potato country. Many of the signs offered tours of factories and farms, potato chip museums, and Florenceville, the French Fry Capital of the World. French fries are the foundation of a dish called poutine, invented in Québec (not entirely sure about that, but it was the first place I encountered it). Au revoir, New Brunswick; we're off to Montréal to try to find out.

Some famous people born in, educated in, housed or claimed by New Brunswick?
Actor Donald Sutherland. Jockey Ron Turcotte. Singer Roch Voisine. Actor Walter Pidgeon. Singer Stompin' Tom Connors. Politician René Levesque.

What to see next time?
Roosevelt Cottage on Campobello Island.

Campbellton, also noted for skiing at nearby Sugarloaf Mountain and for Atlantic salmon fishing, honored downtown with a sculpture of a giant leaping salmon, more than twenty-seven feet tall and made of stainless steel.

What to see more of?
The Fredericton riverfront.

What to see less of?
Bugs—although, let's face it, where are you going to go, anywhere in summer, and not have to think, at least a little bit, about insects? Okay, not San Francisco (and not Vancouver or Victoria). But not everyone has this issue;

Zig never seems to notice them. But if you are like me, just take along some repellent, and be grateful whenever you are in a spot where they don't seem to congregate.

Surprises?
Two people born in New Brunswick that I had not known about: former Québec Premier René Levesque (in Campbellton) and poet Bliss Carman (in Fredericton).

GAIL HULNICK

Chapter Five

QUÉBEC

Je me souviens

I am open-minded about many things, but I had to work to add poutine to the list of exceptional cuisine. This dish originated in Québec, La Belle Province, and now is popular all over the world. It has evolved beyond its simple beginnings as a layered plate of French fries, cheese curds, and brown gravy.

Québec is about many things, but one of the most important is food. You can find fine French cuisine, pizza, bannock, and poutine ... and you should try to find them all. At least once. When I was a kid, I had my first bowl of French onion soup in Québec and I've never forgotten it. Nor has it ever been equaled. I had my first taste of tortière (also spelled tourtière) there, a meat pie dish that originated in Québec and features a mixture of beef and pork sautéed with a careful blend of spices, then baked in a flaky pastry shell. I served it as a traditional Christmas Eve dish for many, many years.

What other foods originated in or are associated with Québec? Tarte au sucre (sugar pie), pea soup, baked beans, cretons (a cold meat spread), and poutine (as I noted earlier) with variations at restaurants and food trucks all over the world that cover everything from sausage, chicken, and bacon, to caviar and truffles.

Other delectable foods associated with Québec: bagels (in Montréal); cheese (in Eastern Townships); tire sur la neige (in the Laurentians—maple syrup poured over fresh snow, forming a sort of flexible, taffy candy); smoked meat sandwiches (in Montréal); and Charlevoix lamb (like French Champagne or Italian Parma ham, only lamb from this specific region east of Québec City can be marketed as Charlevoix lamb, since 2009).

Québec has its poutine ... what have the other provinces contributed? Newfoundland, its codfish; P.E.I., its potatoes; New Brunswick, its fiddleheads; Ontario, its BeaverTails; Manitoba, its Winnipeg goldeye; Saskatchewan, its Saskatoon berry pie; Alberta, its barbecued beef and Taber corn; and B.C., its Nanaimo Bars, a dessert that can, if nobody's looking, become your appetizer and entrée, too.

This discussion of food feels like an appropriate moment to recall one of my favorite quotations about writing, from Anaïs Nin: "We write to taste life twice, in the moment and in retrospect." This is true of any kind of writing, but it is particularly true of travel writing. It derives from the same motivation to capture an experience and a place as photography does, in the instant after seeing, or as painting does, taking many hours, days, months, even years. Travel writers also reflect and dissect the moments they've had in strange, new places. Reflect, examine, and, as Anaïs Nin writes, taste. In the case of Québec, I've often enjoyed the pleasures of remembering, of savoring and tasting past moments there, and of trying to capture them in words.

We crossed from New Brunswick into Québec on Day Six of our journey and gained an hour. Québec is the province that puts you into a new time zone, Eastern Standard Time. At the time of year for this trip, in August, it was Eastern Daylight Time, actually, which would turn to Standard Time in the fall when the clocks are turned back an hour.

Canada has five time zones. Five and a half, in a way, as I've mentioned previously. That should give you an idea of the width of the thing—there are some time zones in Europe that have twenty countries in them! (Okay, so I exaggerate. My point is made, anyway. Canada is a big country.) The time zones are Pacific, Mountain, Central,

Eastern, and Atlantic. Then we have Newfoundland and Labrador, which have the time set half an hour later than the time in the Atlantic time zone. That's why you might, in airports and elsewhere, see clocks with a hand on the twelve and the other, the 'big' hand, on the six.

So far on this trip, I've been in the Newfoundland and Labrador time zone, then the Atlantic, for Nova Scotia, Prince Edward Island, and New Brunswick. For Québec and Ontario, it will be Eastern time, and when I checked my messages I could see from the new time that my smartphone had set automatically. You gotta love technology.

I could also tell that I was into new terrain because the road signs had changed. Many of them were exclusively in French now. In New Brunswick, they were in French and in English. I know what you are thinking: "Do I have to learn a new language if I want to go to Québec? Or at least buy a really good phrase book? Or install a translation app on my phone?"

Okay, maybe I don't know what you were thinking. But it's not a bad question, n'est-ce pas? Quesque c'est les différences principales au Québec? Pas toute la province—c'est un autre livre. Je parle seulement d'un road trip.

I really didn't see that many road signs that I couldn't figure out, thanks to either the idiot-proof pictograms or the symbols that are common no matter what country or language you are driving in. A little bit of high-school French from back in the day helped too. I saw one sign that read "8h à 19h Lun à Ven". That would be 8:00 a.m. to 7:00 p.m. (the twenty-four hour clock) Monday to Friday (lundi à vendredi). "Signalisation métrique" is one that you see posted near the U.S. border to remind drivers that Canada is on the metric system.

In indigenous or First Nations territory you might see both a native language and French or English. In some locations, usually with place names, only indigenous words will be used.

I came across a few traffic rules in Québec, and in other provinces, that differ from those in the U.S. This might be a good spot to observe that studying up on the rules for each place ahead of time isn't a bad idea, if you want to be 100 percent certain that you are avoiding any possible fines or tickets.

The left lane of the highway, for example. In many places, you'll see signs reminding you that the left-most lane is supposed to be a passing lane, but in Québec they have a ticket and a fine ready to hand you if they catch you pulling into the left lane and then just cruising along there. It's a passing lane; you're supposed to get out of it and back over to the right, even if there is no other vehicle anywhere near you and even if you are traveling at the speed limit precisely. You also can't pass on the right on Québec highways.

If you have to go slower than the speed limit, you're supposed to put on your four-way flashers. Motorcycles can't ride side-by-side in a single lane. Same thing for groups of cyclists, and a group can't be any bigger than fifteen cyclists.

You can't leave a child under seven alone in a vehicle without an adult, even if you think they're buckled in safely, you'll only be gone to pick up something in the store for a minute, your eleven-year-old is right there to keep an eye on things in the car, and other unacceptable arguments.

There are big fines for texting or talking on a cell phone while driving a vehicle, even if you're stopped at a traffic light.

After crossing the border from New Brunswick, the road signage change was the first thing I noticed. Next it was the landscape. I could still see the rolling hills, the open spaces, the fertile farmland ... but it seemed more populated. There were more farmhouses, more vehicles on the road, more activity off in the distance.

Is this an accurate perception? A little online research brought me the following 2017 population numbers: 8.39 million in Québec; 759,665 in New Brunswick; 953,669 in Nova Scotia; 528,817 in Newfoundland and Labrador; and 152,021in Prince Edward Island.

There you go.

So, yes, my impression is quite accurate.

Just to be complete: Ontario has a population of 14.19 million, Manitoba 1.33 million, Saskatchewan 1.16 million,

Alberta 4.28 million, and British Columbia 4.81 million.

And just for comparison's sake: the population of Nunavut is 37,996; Northwest Territories is 44,520; and Yukon is 38,459.

Total population of Canada: 36,708,083 people.

Most of them live in or near the cities that cluster in the southern parts of the country and near the Trans-Canada Highway that I followed on this trip. That's not an absolute or perfect description; there are plenty of population centers that have grown up around other highways, for many reasons. There are also many thousands of miles of open, empty country. I covered some of them, but I didn't even begin to explore the wilderness that is this country.

Enough statistics. It's time to listen to some music. I put on Celine Dion and stared out the window at the passing landscape, thinking back on my history with Québec. I've seen it in winter, summer, fall, and spring; and I've seen both the big cities and the tiny towns. I agree with those who say it's the closest you get to a European feel in North America, with the air filled with the sounds of the French language and the architecture telling the story of explorers and settlers from three and four hundred years ago. I've been there so many times and it has such a lot of meaning to me that thoughts of the controversies and issues, the divisions and long-held grudges just leave me feeling incredibly sad.

It's far beyond my capabilities to describe or summarize the history of Québec in Canada. This is not a book about politics, anyway, and I would urge you, if your interests skew in that direction, to find other books and other writers. An evasion? Yes, probably. But detachment often leads to wisdom, and that's what I'm after. I have no idea what the answers are to the monumental questions facing Québec and Canada, but I would like to continue to grope my way toward them. I believe that the more time I spend talking and the less I spend listening and questioning, on major matters of politics or philosophy, the less likely it is that I will ever have an answer.

So after half an hour of wrestling with what I might write, if anything, about the weightier aspects of Québec life, I decided on 'nothing', and turned up the volume on the music player. Celine Dion is brilliant. I saw her perform live once, in Las Vegas, and it is a peak memory. Recordings are to be treasured, yes, but seeing a musician doing her thing on stage is an experience in a class all its own.

One of my other live-performance favorites from Québec is music in the traditional style, doing the old songs, fingers flying on a fiddle while the shoes tap on a wooden plank, occasionally a chanson à répondre. It's very similar to music you'll hear in parts of Louisiana. One thing I always enjoy when watching a live performance is the moment when two musicians catch one another's eye because they are in perfect sync and everything is just so tasty. There is always a smile. With traditional Québec music, the performers smile nonstop!

As I rode along enjoying the music, we passed a sign announcing the town of Saint Louis-du-Ha! Ha!

Really? Is this for real? Look this up!

Not now though. I've had to curb my habit of jumping on my phone the minute I have a chance. Nobody wants to cause an eight-car pileup just because they have to know right now the name of that actor playing the fourth character to get killed in the third episode of *Game of Thrones*. But you also don't want to have your nose down and your eyes on a phone screen constantly when you're on a road trip you've been dreaming about for years. So I kept a list of 'things to look up', and that became part of the nightly routine, after the miles and kilometers were clocked and the hours recorded.

Our route took us along the south shore of the Saint Lawrence River, where the Trans-Canada Highway was built close enough that you can see the water as you pass by.

I fell asleep after lunch and missed a few hours of the day's travel, so I was not qualified to comment much on the things we passed on the way to Montréal. At least, that's what Zig says. He says what I missed were the farms, some of them created hundreds of years ago. They are long narrow strips of land, running from the waterfront to the highway so that as many farmers as possible had access to the river, a vital link to markets and to the rest of the world.

Québec, like all of the other provinces, is a fascinating mix of rural and urban experience. Brilliant writers, including Mordecai Richler, Roch Carrier, Marie-Claire Blais, and Anne Hébert, have rendered the stories of the people in vivid and memorable detail. A quotation from Carrier's *Le Chandail de Hockey (The Hockey Sweater)* is on the back of some of the Canadian five-dollar bills: "The winters of my childhood were long, long seasons. We lived in three places—the school, the church, and the skating rink—but our real life was on the skating rink."

And in Québec's official language: «Les hivers de mon enfance étaient des saisons, longues, longues. Nous vivions en trois lieux: l'école, l'église et la patinoire; mais la vraie vie était sur la patinoire.»

We had a pleasant drive, and then we hit the Montréal traffic. Yuck! Coming toward the city from Longueil and Drummondville, it took two hours to go ten miles. There was no sign of an accident. Not that that would have speeded things up in any way, it just would have made me feel less frustrated. Somehow, unexplained inconvenience is worse. All I could see, though, were multiple lanes of traffic merging and crawling, inch by inch, into an endless horizon.

Finally, we emerged into Port Champlain, where the freeway ends and the traffic pours into a residential street. The highway flow suddenly faced the impediments of traffic lights and stop signs, but we had been moving so slowly it didn't matter. The scene was complicated by many construction machines, workers, and signs. Yes, I know I did say earlier that I wanted to see evidence of effort being expended to fix potholes and keep roads in good repair, and I know that doesn't happen by magic.

But could it happen late at night when there is hardly any traffic? Or at least happen at some time of the day when it's not going to inconvenience me?

Some local friends say they avoid Montréal if they possibly can, and I suppose that's an alternative if you've been there multiple times and don't care if you go back. But on this cross-Canada journey, Montréal was in the plan and other than being dropped down into the middle of it via parachute, I couldn't see a way around the need to endure this traffic.

Downtown is not easy for out-of-towners either. I'm not saying 'don't go there'; I'm just suggesting you be prepared, mentally. It's particularly tough with a car. Parking is as scarce as a moose in Newfoundland. We found our hotel easily, thanks to Carmen, our GPS, but the assigned parking space was four blocks away, at the end of an alley, with poor signage leading to it and a bumpy laneway to pull rollerboard suitcases over on the way back from it to the hotel.

It had to get better than this.

And of course, it did. Montréal is one of my favorite cities in the world and inside half an hour my mood was much improved. The city has a buzz of energy that is unique; that's one of the main reasons I love it. It's also visually entrancing, in different ways, at different times of the year. In July, the streets, the homes and businesses, and the parks all glow with the colors and sunshine of summer; in December, it's all still there but with the shimmer of snow and frost decorating every roof, every doorway, and every tree for winter. It has a sense of style, sophistication, and design similar to what you find in the great cities of Italy, and yet it is Montréal, exceptional and inimitable.

This year the city was celebrating its 375th anniversary. In 1642, Roman Catholic missionaries from France set up a mission there, dedicated to the Virgin Mary, making it one of the oldest settlements of European people on the continent.

We went out to look for dinner, so tired from the long day in the car and so much time jammed in traffic gridlock that we didn't range far afield. We considered a sidewalk café near the hotel and a fine-dining restaurant nearby but then went for a pizza place instead. Even a pizza place in Montréal is something special. The wine is treated as something special, the pizza is not like anything you'd find in any chain restaurant in any one of a hundred cities or towns, and the servers who bring it to you look as though they belong in a fashion magazine.

On the street you see so many beautiful people, so much style and fashion. A lot of smokers, though. Too bad. The walk back took us along Sherbrooke Street, which had been turned into an open-air museum as part of the celebration of the city's 375th anniversary. Beautiful statues and parks greeted us after every turn of every corner; truly, this is a walker's city.

The groundbreaking travel writer Richard Halliburton wrote in the 1920s, "Let those who wish have their respectability. I wanted freedom, freedom to indulge in whatever caprice struck my fancy, freedom to search in the farthermost corners of the earth for the beautiful, the joyous, and the romantic." Montréal is one of the beautiful, joyous, and romantic corners.

We stayed out as long as possible because there was nothing nearly so attractive back at the hotel. It was an average layout in an old building with a funky smell. Later, the clock radio came on unexpectedly, waking me and telling me in a loud male voice in French that it was 3:45 a.m. Alors, merci bien. Yes, a bit early. It's an energetic city, but that was a bit much.

After such a wakeful night, a high-protein breakfast would be the perfect launch for the next day's travel to Toronto. Does anybody eat poutine for breakfast?

Some famous people born in, educated in, housed or claimed by Québec?
Prime Ministers Pierre Trudeau, Justin Trudeau, Brian Mulroney, Jean Chretien. Actor William Shatner. Race car drivers Gilles and Jacques Villeneuve. Actor Glenn Ford. Author and singer-songwriter Leonard Cohen. Astronaut Marc Garneau. Writer Gabrielle Roy. Hockey players Guy Lafleur, Patrick Roy, 'Boom Boom' Geoffrion, and many others.

What to see next time?
Québec City and the area north of it. We gave this a miss this time because we've been there in the past, but it is a lovely part of the province, with its breathtaking scenery, covered bridges, picturesque towns and villages. On a return visit, this region would be the top of the list.

The hike to the top of Mount Royal. This walk begins right near the middle of the city, by McGill University, where both of my daughters went to school, and takes you up to an amazing view.

What to see more of?
La cuisine française. We had a nice dinner but more time, more meals, more restaurants would have been high priority if I'd decided to spend more time in La Belle Province.

What to see less of?
The traffic around Montréal. We know several people who won't go near the city anymore because of the terrible driving experiences. I have no idea what engineering feats would be necessary to improve the flow, and I don't know the ins and outs of all of the causes of the mess. Just fix it!

Surprises?
How reluctant I was to leave. Perhaps it was because of the two hours we spent stuck in a traffic jam, trying to get into Montréal, I felt so invested that I wanted to stay much longer, to get a 'return'. Perhaps it was because downtown Montréal is just so vibrant and alive, I wanted to stay and just walk it, from one end to another, again and again.

Our noble steed, pulled to the side of the road in the mountains of western Alberta. Reliable, comfortable and even a little sporty, he took us the entire journey without incident. We sadly parted ways at the end of the trip.

On April 12, 1980 Terry Fox began his journey at the waterfront of St. John's, Newfoundland. His Marathon of Hope inspires millions of Canadians to this day. The Zig and I shared his starting point for our own cross-country adventure.

The ferry crossing from North Sydney, Nova Scotia to Argentia, Newfoundland and Labrador took about 16 hours. Depending on the weather and the time of year you might see sunset, sunrise, dolphins, whales, ocean-going ships or, alternately, nothing but fog.

The lighthouse at Cape Spear, Newfoundland and Labrador. This is as easternmost as it gets. Nothing out there till Europe.

Waiting to board the ferry at the dock in North Sydney, Nova Scotia. Vagabonds and vehicles from every corner of the continent, I would love to know their stories!

Mountie or hockey player. For a moment, waiting for the ferry, you can occupy either of these quintessential Canadian occupations.

The lighthouse in Peggy's Cove, Nova Scotia. The windshield view was oddly reminiscent of so many of my days driving in and around Vancouver.

The hills and lakes of Cape Breton, Nova Scotia. Go straight, go straight, go straight...

The countless fishing villages strung along the rocky coastline of Nova Scotia are impossibly quaint and picturesque. I understand that the view in February can be slightly different!

Yes, it has gables and yes, they are green. The actual home that is the setting for *Anne of Green Gables* in Prince Edward Island is also a magnet for busloads of tourists.

Confederation Bridge—Canada's longest—connects the mainland in New Brunswick to Prince Edward Island. In a Hotel California-esque manner, the $47 toll must be paid if you want to leave the island. It's an extra $40 if you're too tense to drive yourself across the 12.9 kilometer span.

Top down on the waterfront in Charlottetown, P.E.I., the 'birthplace of Confederation.' The city is familiar to every Canadian school kid.

1,282 feet of antique pragmatism across the Saint John River. It provides a handy dallying spot for young lovers looking to steal a kiss and it keeps the snow off the road.

The world famous Magnetic Hill, in Moncton, New Brunswick. Supposedly it doesn't work if your car is made of plastic.

Culture, the arts, high fashion, diversity—it's all around you in downtown Montréal. There is no law requiring graffiti to be in French.

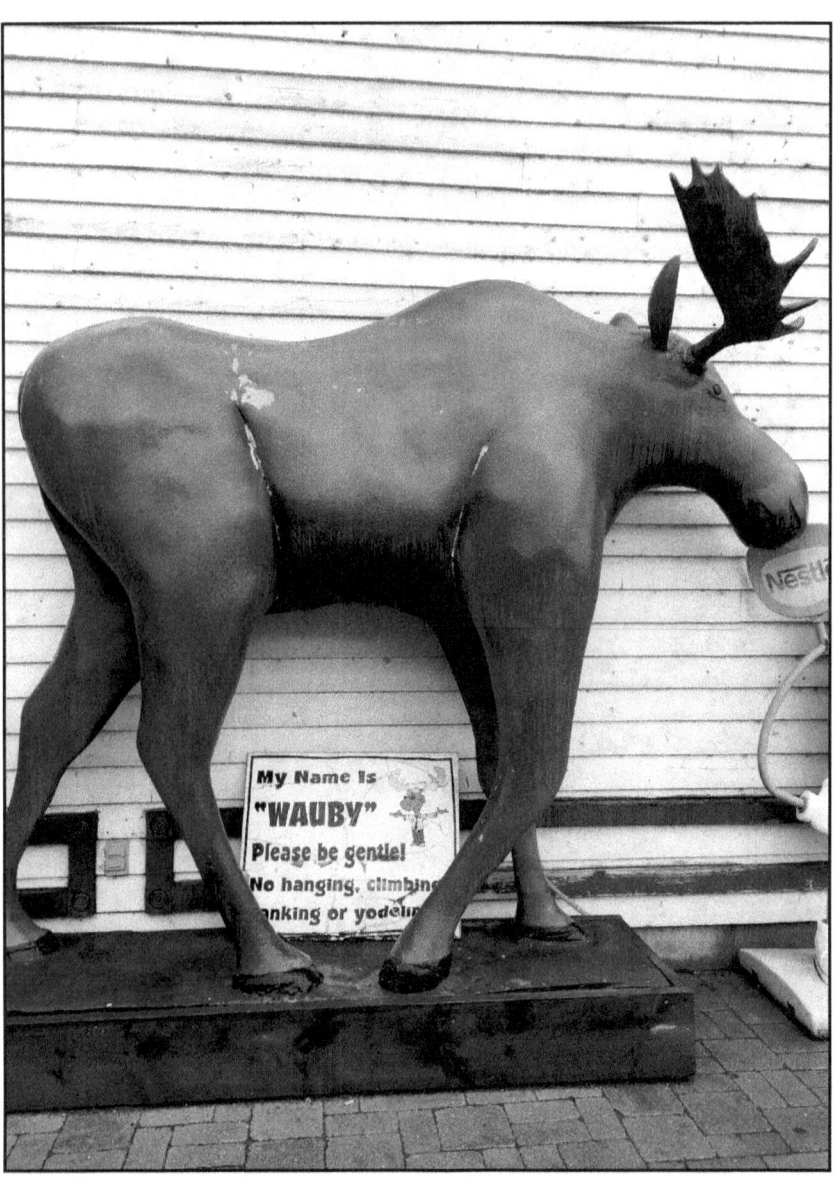

All the way to Muskoka, Ontario and still no photo of a live moose. Sensing the halfway point of our odyssey approaching, I resorted to taking pictures of anything that resembled one.

The Gardiner Expressway, circa 1962 and the Toronto skyline, circa 2017. Somehow they manage to keep it working.

The most recent of a long line of goose statues on the side of the Trans-Canada Highway in Wawa, Ontario is one of the most photographed landmarks in North America. The first, erected in 1963, was made of plaster and didn't last long in the northern Ontario weather.

The Canadian Museum for Human Rights, located near The Forks in downtown Winnipeg, Manitoba, is the first new Canadian national museum since 1967 and the first ever to be located outside the national capital region in Ottawa.

The little park and stream in Winnipeg
where some of us played on the way
to school way back when. Thankfully,
other than the trees growing larger, some
things haven't changed much.

The staff at the Hotel Saskatchewan in Regina felt that the Zig and I could use a little recognition for our efforts. That, and a night in The Premier's Suite, made us feel pretty darn special.

Not to be outdone by its siblings in Ontario and British Columbia, the City of Regina wants to show the world that it can do an impressive skyline too. Where's the birthday cake?

Miles and miles of miles and miles. The wheatfields across the Saskatchewan prairie extend to the horizon and then just keep on going.

Eight provinces down, and two to go. By this point we'd completely exhausted our supply of superlatives.

Back in the day, there used to be grain elevators across Alberta. And back in the day, as a young TV news reporter, I would freeze my fingers off doing an on-location report while pretending to be comfortable.

An hour or so west of Red Deer, Alberta, we caught our first glimpse of the mountains. There is no mistaking this for Peggy's Cove. Or Montréal. Or Muskoka. Or a wheat field in Saskatchewan. This is one really impressive country!
(Note the rumble strip along the shoulder)

In and around the breathtaking town of Banff, Alberta, you'll find the perfect playground for skiers, hikers, climbers, mountain bikers... Oh, and bears.

East coast, west coast, it doesn't matter. They both have an endless supply of impossibly pretty coves and inlets. This one can be seen when you visit Butchart Gardens just outside Victoria, British Columbia.

Vancouver may not have invented the glass-and-steel skyline. But it has worked pretty hard to perfect it. The views of Stanley Park, the North Shore, the Fraser Valley and Vancouver Island from these penthouses is spectacular. (When it's not raining!)

Start at 'Mile 0.' Travel almost 8,000 kilometers.
End at 'Mile 0'.
Hey, this is Canada. What can I say?

Chapter Six

ONTARIO

"You always miss one hundred percent of the shots you don't take." - Wayne Gretzky

This is probably one of the most famous quotes about sports ever given by a Canadian athlete ... and perhaps one of the most famous quotes about sports, period.

Yet, having watched hockey's Greatest for decades and interviewed him once or twice, I'm gonna guess that he didn't mean it all that profoundly when he first said it. It was just the truth, literally; if you don't take a shot, you have no chance. It's obvious; what's so cloud-clearing about that?

In Ontario, they don't spend a lot of time not taking a shot. It is Canada's most populous province and the home to both its biggest city (Toronto) and its capital city (Ottawa).

Southern Ontario is where I spent five of my most important years, in high school and in first-year university. Then I was away for thirty-five years, moving to finish university and to begin a journalism career. My recent return trips had involved planes and trains (no automobiles). I was looking forward to seeing what had changed and what I remembered.

After the stop in Montréal and the drive through Québec, we crossed into Ontario and followed the highway near Kingston. Kingston is the location of one of the best universities in Canada. Many of my close friends attended Queens, as did my son. The city itself is one of the best examples of Canada as it was in the 1870s; many of the old buildings and the old neighborhoods have been preserved.

Driving the Trans-Canada Highway, you would stay to the north, and visit Ottawa, Canada's capital city. Been there many times, winter and summer, and it's quite different, depending when you go. On Canada Day, flowers and blossoms abound. In January or February, the temperatures can hit minus forty and the walks outdoors involve half a block, half a dozen careful inhalations of frosty air, and a thankful arrival at whatever indoor destination you had in mind. During Winterlude, though, this annual multi-week outdoors party has the residents and visitors to Ottawa-Gatineau embracing the season rather than shrinking from it.

The occupants of Ottawa were a major part of my life in the late seventies and eighties, when I was covering politics, and it would have been interesting to see the city again. But on this trip, I had decided to take several detours off the Trans-Canada and in Ontario, I was going south to visit family and friends in Toronto.

This highway from Montréal to Toronto was one I drove or was driven on quite a few times when I was in high school at Erindale Secondary School in Mississauga, Ontario—for family trips, for school trips, and for a very special girlfriends' trip to Carnival in Québec City when I was seventeen. My first observation was that the increase in the quantity of vehicles has been absolutely exponential.

As the miles and the hundreds of trucks rolled by, I realized that many other things had changed. I recalled many of the place names but not many of the landmarks or even the scenery. A lot of years had passed—enough, I think, that I was arriving here as a newcomer. I had expected this province in particular (other than British Columbia where I lived for thirty-three years) would look the most familiar. Instead it seemed strange. But as Robert Louis Stevenson wrote, "There are no foreign lands. It is the traveler only who is foreign."

We spent almost four days crossing Ontario, plus a

few more in Toronto. The Montréal to Toronto leg is about 475 kilometers. We started out in a heavy rainstorm, with thunder and lightning. Outside Montréal, we passed through the suburbs of Pointe-Claire and Beaconsfield and I remembered high school days in Mississauga, just west of Toronto, being one of the new kids, meeting new friends who had just arrived from Point-Claire and Dollard des Ormeaux. These were such exotic names for a girl from the prairies, even one who had spent a few years in Winnipeg, which has its own historical connection with French Canada. The touches there were light and fleeting, nothing as immediate as this, though.

As I rode along near the tracks through southern Ontario I thought about how, for many, the big dream is a trip across Canada by train, done to the soundtrack of Gordon Lightfoot's "Canadian Railroad Trilogy." But the reality is that a lot of that dream will unfold while riding very slowly through back yards, though the slummy parts of towns, slowing down even more to let other trains go by and not being able to spontaneously choose a diversion or digression. If your destination is direct and simple, a train trip is fantastic, especially if you've been able to avoid airport parking, checking in, security clearance, boarding lounge boredom, or highway congestion. I've taken quite a few trips by rail between Toronto and Montréal, and it's particularly efficient in the winter when the train ploughs through the snow, and you have no responsibility for the safety or forward progress of your car on a day full of post-blizzard challenges like snow drifts and black ice.

This Ontario landscape in August looked nothing like a winter experience. The green hills and farms we passed were lovely. 'Tidy' was the word that came to mind: farmhouses with not a shingle or board out of place, yards empty of any obsolete vehicles or abandoned tools, fields framed by fences built at perfect right angels to one another. We were just across the lake from the U.S., and yet somehow it never crossed my mind at any point in this part of the road trip. Perhaps it was because of all that Canadian road and muskeg we'd traversed in the ten days up to now, but I felt a long way away from America.

I felt the same way as a kid, I didn't have the freedom

to visit the U.S. whenever I wanted. We didn't do it frequently as a family; I think it was perhaps twice in the five years we lived in central Canada before returning to the west—once to Virginia Beach and once to Myrtle Beach. We stayed long enough to drop some (Canadian) dollars in gas stations, motels, restaurants, and souvenir shops. When I look at the map now, and really study it, as I never did in those days, I realize that I had no perception of how close we lived to America.

I grew up in Mississauga, just west of Toronto, in a time when, although we were proud of the 'Canadian mosaic', we hadn't yet welcomed as many immigrants to the country. The whole area was a lot more rural then, and the local shopping mall was the magnet for all kids over sixteen with a driver's license and a borrowed station wagon.

As we sped along the highway past Scarborough, farther east, the familiar sights of Toronto came into view.. There is the sign for Yonge Street, Toronto's main street and the longest street in the world, when you follow it along Highway 11. Its end point is the waterfront of Lake Ontario.

We drove downtown and, on either side of the freeway, green glass towers loomed into the sky. I thought of "Emerald City" as we passed by them. Toronto has an even better nickname nowadays, though; Drake, the Toronto-born singer, celebrated from New York to L.A., has dubbed it The Six, referring to the telephone prefix.

We had dinner downtown on Front Street near St. Lawrence Market. In Ontario, foodies look for pasta on College Street West, ice wine on the Niagara peninsula, Windsor-style pizza, with its thick crust and extra-extra-extra-extra cheese, and Ottawa BeaverTails, a trademarked snack made of fried dough stretched to resemble the tail of a beaver.

Three days of visiting family and friends and then we headed out on the road again, this time going north toward Sudbury. The online map said four hours but it ended up being six. This often happens, but I think this time I could link it pretty clearly to the heavy traffic leaving the city. All these people and vehicles were heading to the Muskoka district, the lake country.

Highway 400 heading north was the next road we traversed, passing hills where I remembered skiing as a teenager and towns with pottery shops where we shopped long ago.

Then we turned on to Highway 69 through Muskoka toward cottage country, the term given this part of northern Ontario by the Toronto people from the south who pour onto the highways in the summer time for a weekend getaway at the cottage. All along the road I saw incredible natural rock formations with red and pink stripes marking the march of time. I also saw hundreds of not-natural rock formations, tiny stacks of rocks and stones built on top of the roadside cliffs, some of them in the shape of the Canadian symbol, the inukshuk. The inukshuk (plural inuksuit) is a stack of rocks and stones originally used by the Inuit and other Arctic peoples as communication and navigation aids. A red one is on the flag of one of the Canadian territories, Nunavut. Many of the other little towers along this road are set up in random and extremely intricate constructions that don't represent an inukshuk, a house, an animal, or anything other than the builder's inspiration. They were all evidence of our fellow and sister travelers, those on foot, leaving something behind, adding to the landscape rather than removing anything from it.

Our stop that night was Sudbury. I couldn't see much of it through the rain and drizzle. It is famous as the location of another outsized road landmark, the Big Nickel, a thirty-foot replica of a 1951 piece of Canadian change, worth five cents. We arrived in fog and rain, and we left that way the next morning. The survival conditions here would have been (and still are, if you're alone) difficult, to say the least.

The next day the destination was Thunder Bay. This was to be one of the longest days—and in fact it turned out to be **the** longest, at 1,024 kilometers and twelve-and-a-half hours. You may have noticed that we haven't had any more of the Miss Hathaway transcriptions of dictated notes from the road. I discovered that my cell phone bill and data usage charges were going to be absolutely astronomical if I continued, so the phone was put away. We were relying on the GPS for directions and although it wasn't quite as entertaining as the mobile phone docs app, it did have its moments, the best one coming when the city of Sault Ste. Marie was mispronounced, repeatedly, as "Salt Sweet Murray", rather than the proper way, "Soo (or 'Sue') Saint Maree".

The highway took us past Webbwood, on the north shore of Georgian Bay, which proudly proclaims itself the home of Canada's first woman mayor, Barbara Manley, elected in 1936.

Massey, Ontario, another ten miles or so on down the road, looked like a lively town. We drove past restored heritage buildings, posters about a street painting festival, and colorful murals on a motel. The central square had a memorial to Terry Fox and his Marathon of Hope.

The homes and businesses through northern Ontario had taken to the 150th celebration as enthusiastically as those in the Maritimes and Newfoundland and Labrador. Flags of all sizes hung and flew from poles, fences, garage doors, barn doors, and windows.

A bit farther on, I got another wonderful addition for my 'great place names' list—Seldom Seen Road. Along this stretch, I saw many places called The Trading Post. There were also a lot of signs advertising 'sign makers available'.

Safety signs were in lavish supply, too. "Please don't feed the bears"; "Don't drink and drive"; "Don't tailgate". There seem to be many more of these than in the States—is Canada that much more protective? More anxious about the traveler's ability to make good decisions?

I also saw many places where French language signs and indigenous language signs were mounted alongside the English ones. If you're ever playing a game of visual trivia, that's a tipoff that you're looking at Canada.

I passed the town of Iron Bridge, on the north shore of Lake Huron, then the community of Huron Shores. On this trip, we would see three of the Great Lakes—Ontario, Huron, and Superior. The Great Lakes are, to the Canadian psyche, what the Grand Canyon is to the American, or Uluru, formerly called Ayers Rock, is to the Australian. This imposing natural geological feature is one of the most commanding aspects of the Canadian map. If you live near any one of them, it is the most significant aspect of your neighborhood weather, real estate prices, and recreation. If you've never seen any of the Lakes or you need some sort of visual reference, you could look up "Group of Seven" online or visit an art gallery where the paintings of Arthur Lismer, A.Y. Jackson, and the others in this group of Canadian landscape artists are exhibited. You'll see the windswept cliffs, the stark trees, and the skies that almost seem to speak, as well as hundreds of other details that defined this school of painting and inspired many travelers to dream of a northern Ontario journey.

The rain and drizzle had eased now and the sky was brightening. Just fifty more klicks to Salt Sweet Murray. (Klick is short for kilometer, and its use began, I'm told, in the military.) Along this side of Lake Superior, the highway hugs it so close that a few hundred yards more and we'd be boating, rather than driving. We passed Batchawana Bay and Pancake Bay on the eastern shore of Lake Superior and then an open expanse. The water had a lot of wave action and chop; it gave me a shiver in the first seconds that I saw it.

We reached the halfway point of the Trans-Canada Highway just north of Sault Ste. Marie and kept on rolling, toward a Friday night in Thunder Bay. There would be four Friday nights on this trip. Last week we were in Corner Brook, Newfoundland and Labrador, and the week before that, the first one of the trip as we headed north from home in Savannah, was in Stafford, Virginia, U.S. Next Friday night we would be in Victoria, B.C.

Americans always ask how cold it is in Canada. In mid-August, in this northern Ontario town in mid-afternoon, the temperature was 63° F. That's about thirty degrees cooler than the average we can expect down south at this time of year.

The landscape was getting wilder, with the trees, rocky shores, hills, and creeks looking more like the scene from a Group of Seven painting every moment. We passed the Williams Mine and then rounded a curve toward Wawa, Ontario. It's a spot that is famous for another of Canada's freakishly large roadside attractions—this one, a goose.

A little farther along and we came to a northern Ontario town dedicated to another wildlife specimen—a very special bear, Winnie the Pooh. In White River, a veterinarian and soldier from Winnipeg bought a bear cub from a trapper and took it with him to England. When Captain Colebourn received the news in 1914 that he would soon be shipping out to France, he arranged for "Winnie" to stay at the London Zoo, where the bear became a favorite with the crowds and the muse for A.A. Milne, who wrote stories about the bear for his son, Christopher Robin, and let the little boy add his pet swan's name, "Pooh", to Winnie's.

Thunder Bay is in the history books as end of the Terry Fox Run. The exact spot on the Trans-Canada Highway had a small sign, then a bit farther on there was a big lookout, set in a majestic spot, in an effort to give recognition here fitting to the inspiration he provided.

The next morning was Day 14 of the cross-country trip. We were leaving Thunder Bay in sunshine and heading for Winnipeg, the capital city of Manitoba, the next province to the west. A sign told us that the Eastern Time Zone ends just near Savonna Portage, north of Thunder Bay. It was a very wide time zone.

Many spots throughout Ontario are named 'portage', after the term for the carrying of a canoe or other boat between two navigable bodies of water or around an obstacle in the water. Historically and present tense, Ontario is crazy about canoes and canoeing.

As we drove through the small community of Upsala, I did a double-take at the sight of their contribution to the world of public art. I'd never seen anything like it.

"Is that a mosquito?" I asked Zig.

He had his attention on the road. "Yeah, I'm pretty sure there are a few mosquitoes around here," he said.

"No, it's a giant one! Look over there."

The sculpture depicts a giant mosquito flying off, carrying a man. Now this was something I had to look up, never mind the data usage charges.

Apparently the town of Upsala commissioned it to show how big the mosquitoes do get. The sculpture also showed the sixteen-foot-long metal insect carrying a knife and fork. Very funny.

We were heading for Dryden now, fifty kilometers away. The trees began looking healthier and taller. The fields beside the highway here weren't sandy any longer; they were green and lush, laden with pretty white and orange wildflowers. It was mostly just miles of emptiness, and I really didn't see many farms or billboards or lakes until we got to Dryden. There were a lot of moose signs but no sign of any moose.

We traveled another one hundred thirty kilometers or so to Kenora, on the edge of the Lake of the Woods region, with its hundreds of thousands of acres of waterfront and fourteen thousand islands. Not much hockey or any winter sports here at this time of year, but we saw boats, ATVs, waterskiing, and fishing gear at every turn.

We started Ontario in the rain and finished the same way. Not that I'm obsessed with the weather, but it's rather fundamental when you're planning and describing a road trip, especially in an unpredictable country like Canada. I've driven through the Rockies in July and encountered a snowstorm. Halloween can be an occasion for a zombie surfer costume, complete with short shorts and flip flops, and other years it can call for a parka. You just almost never know.

Some famous people born in, educated in, housed or claimed by Ontario?
Besides Winnie the Pooh, actor/comedian Mike Myers. Author Margaret Atwood. Businessman Galen Weston. Actor/businessman Dan Aykroyd. Singer Gord Downie. Author Lawrence Hill.

What to see next time?
Rouge National Urban Park. This park in the eastern area of Toronto, Markham, Pickering, and Uxbridge is the largest urban park on the continent, twenty-two times larger than Central Park in New York.

What to see more of?

Continuing on the 'park' theme, the Lake of the Woods was definitely an area we could have explored further.

What to see less of?
Muskeg.

Surprises?
The evidence of the diversity of language and culture. Since I lived there in the seventies the population growth has been significant and the change in the composition of the towns and cities has been dramatic.

Chapter Seven

MANITOBA

Portage and Main

The weather is a little less unpredictable in Manitoba, in February. You can bet the farm that it will be cold. Manitoba is known for many things, most of them associated with cold weather, snow, and ice. Yes, of course it has a summer time, but if we are talking superlatives and extremes, it is the winter associations that give Manitoba and its capital city Winnipeg their major shine. Lowest temperatures, heaviest snowfall, longest stretch of freezing weather. The color that comes to mind is white.

Hey, that raises a question—what color is best associated with all the other provinces? Here are my thoughts; feel free to disagree. Newfoundland: Yellow (for the rain gear). Prince Edward Island: Green (for the Gables). Nova Scotia: Silver (for the famous Bluenose schooner that is on the 'tails' side of the Canadian dime and for the weathered shingles on the sides of the buildings). New Brunswick: Red (for the fall foliage and the maple trees). Quebec: Blue (for the background on the flag, behind the fleur-de-lis). Ontario: Also Blue (for the Great Lakes). Manitoba: White (as noted previously, for the weather). Saskatchewan: Gold (for the wheat fields). Alberta: Pink (for the wild rose, its provincial flower). British Columbia: Also Green (for the rainforest).

Besides the weather, we have a lot of things to chat about in Manitoba. Professional hockey—many players were born or raised there (although not as many as in Saskatchewan).

Manitoba also has produced a lot of actors: Anna Paquin, Nia Vardalos, Tina Keeper, Ross Petty, Donnelly Rhodes, Tom Jackson, David Steinberg, Monty Hall. Assembling this list makes me want to find a collective noun for a group of actors, like a pod of whales, a gaggle of geese, or a convocation of eagles. I suppose it would be a 'cast', a 'troupe', or a 'company'. Perhaps an 'ensemble'? A 'team'? A 'dream'?

Winnipeg also is known for brilliant writers Carol Shields and Gabriel Roy; musicians Randy Bachman, Burton Cummings, and Neil Young; and artist William Kurelek.

At the Ontario/Manitoba border, I saw an abrupt change to 'flat'. It was almost instantaneous—one minute I was riding along looking a few hundred yards out at muskeg and rock formations, feeling a gentle slope in the road here and there, turning the wheel, straightening out. The next, I was looking at miles and miles of a level, unchanging plane. Plain, actually—this is the eastern edge of what has been known in the U.S. as the Great Plains. In Canada, we call it 'the Prairies', but it's essentially the same thing.

If mountainous or rugged terrain makes you feel confined, this is the place for you. The horizon appeared to be so far away that I couldn't even really see it. Space, that's what you have here. Open space. Room to move.

East of Winnipeg, coming in from Ontario, you cross an area that is weekend camping territory for the city people. It is one of the popular spots, anyway; people also like to go north, to Riding Mountain National Park and to Winnipeg Beach (which isn't actually in Winnipeg).

I was aware that the trip from from here to British Columbia would take us only along the very edges of what is Canada, in this region (I suppose you can say that about almost any road). The Trans-Canada skirts the southern edge of each of the three prairie provinces—Manitoba, Saskatchewan, and Alberta—and an in-depth exploration of the region and this province would take me far off this beaten track. There simply was not enough time for it on this trip. I admit I am sometimes envious of those full-time travelers who just move (slowly) from place to place, investigating whatever glorious view or fascinating dwelling place takes their fancy. I met a couple on the Newfoundland ferry who had sold their house in Michigan in favor of full-time living in a camper van and were counting up the days until they reached a full year. "A year, at least," she specified, and I didn't doubt for a minute that they could live that way. That kind of time would certainly let you get beyond the single, most commonly used lane through a province or a state, but this time, with three weeks at my disposal, the Trans-Canada and the southerly route were to be the plan.

Winnipeg is at a beautiful confluence of rivers, the Seine, the Assiniboine, and the Red River. One of its highlights is a development called The Forks. It resembles Granville Island in Vancouver or St. Lawrence Market in Toronto, but is unique, of course, as each of these shopping areas is. The Forks is a vibrant collection of hotels, restaurants, shopping magnets, and the newest national museum in Canada, the Canadian National Museum for Human Rights, which draws together exhibits covering seven floors, housed in an unusual building that I thought resembled a Roman soldier's helmet and the Zig thought looked like a stack of napkins. It rose from the banks of the river, in the midst of the color and activity of The Forks, and it almost seemed to throb with purpose and positive energy. Yes, it had some incredibly thought-provoking exhibits, about the Nazi scourge of Europe, the appalling tragedy of slavery, and the Rwandan genocide, to name just a few. It did not engage in false boosterism, but dealt with Canada's less than perfect track record, too, with floor- and brain-space devoted to the treatment of the indigenous peoples and the incarceration of Japanese-Canadians during World War II. But as visitors walk through, from the top floor toward the ground, the story became brighter, and human achievements in making things better were not overlooked.

Winnipeg and Manitoba make a celebration of their climate. This area, The Forks, features the longest naturally frozen skating trail in the world. The Rideau Canal in

Ottawa is often hailed as an another amazing example of using what you get, in winter, and I would argue that skating there and enjoying Winterlude is one of the best things about Canada. But the river area at The Forks would be on that list as well.

Winnipeg has the sunshine, too, and although the girls don't all get so tanned, they also rarely get seasonal affective disorder from gloomy skies from October through May. On a bright, sunny February day in Winnipeg, when the blue sky is the shade of a robin's egg and the light fills your eyes and makes you smile, you could stay outside for hours. Just make sure you have three or four layers on, over your skin, and a toque on your head.

When I was growing up in 'Winterpeg', this fact of February life crashed into the gender discrimination of the day at my school. We were wearing uniforms in those days, even though it was a public, not a private school, and on a frosty day the unfairness was obvious. Rather than the uniform pants required for boys, the girls were required to wear kilts. Even with tights (in the proper color, of course, and only the brand allowed by the school), your legs were freezing. One day it led to a revolt; the jungle telegraph started buzzing one night, via telephone, and the message was passed along—the next day, we all showed up at school wearing pants. What were they going to do, suspend every one of us?

I recall that the principal and other powers-that-be recognized that the rebellion had nothing to do with fashion or vanity and everything to do with not freezing to death. We were given permission to wear pants in the winter, and school in Winnipeg became a bit more bearable.

Winnipeg has been promoted over the years as home to "the coldest spot in North America", the intersection of Portage Avenue and Main Street. I'm not sure whether that is true or not, but people think it is, and it would certainly be close. I lived in Winnipeg for five years and it is the coldest place I've been. Portage and Main is a tourist stop all its own and business people who can't free up much time, outside their meetings, phone calls, and site visits, often make a point of at least passing by Portage and Main, or directing the taxi driver to go past that corner.

This trip we rode through Portage and Main, and past the Manitoba Legislature Building, with Manitoba's best-known symbol, the Golden Boy statue at the top. This seventeen-foot gold statue of the Roman messenger god Mercury, is set facing north at the very top of the dome and was a gift from France in the early twentieth century. Many neighborhoods of the city are leafy and green, with solemn, dignified trees and streets full of charm.

I decided to drive out to Assiniboia, an area in the western part of the city where I lived as a young teenager. As the streets went by, the memories drifted back. Many of them involved walking. Walking from Polo Park, the shopping mall, having been given permission to be out alone for the first time. Taking part in twenty-five mile walkathons, to raise funds from sponsors at ten cents a mile. Carrying a placard and marching in support of Pierre Trudeau, the Kennedys, the 'women's libbers', and against violence and war. Dancing at 'sock hops', listening to the Squires and to Chad Allen and the Expressions (later known as The Guess Who).

The neighborhood looked much the same as it did, although the houses looked a lot smaller to me now. The trees were a lot larger and that was not just a matter of perception. The streets had been transformed by the mature landscaping and what had looked like an ordinary suburb had become quite beautiful. Plant a tree now, everyone.

The roads were quite bumpy in Winnipeg, and the potholes were killer. It was a much smoother ride once we got out onto the highway. The countryside was incredibly flat—a word I am sure I will be using repeatedly, now that we were headed into the prairies portion of the trip.

We stopped just outside Brandon to get lunch at an A&W. I hadn't stopped at many of these fast food chain places because it was always more interesting to check out some of the local spots. But every once in a while . . .

The menu, as in most of these spots, was printed all over the wall. There was no information about nutritional contents and calorie counts, as is required in many parts of the States now, but I was happy to see that a veggie burger was an option. At least, the wall said so; the clerk behind the counter did not.

"You want what?" She was willing to be helpful.

Despite it being on the menu on the wall, and despite it being a relatively simple and common variation from the standard cheese, hamburger, bun, and fried potatoes offered everywhere in the world, the veggie burger stumped the server. She spoke into the little microphone in front of her mouth, calling her supervisor; after a consultation, during which they realized that the request was not for a baby burger but was for a veggie burger, the hunt was on. After about five minutes she emerged, shaking her head.

"We don't do veggie burgers."

The mozza sticks had to do.

There wasn't much here, in this part of southern Manitoba just west of Winnipeg, for the outdoorsman or woman. No signs of lakes or rivers, and I guessed you had to go farther north for that. I saw a few working oil derricks and knew that that there were many more to come, in Alberta, two provinces over. Many of the place names had the French flavor I'd seen in New Brunswick and Ontario, and my nodding acquaintance with Manitoba history gave me to understand that the early forays from France had had lasting impacts, at least on the geographic vocabulary here. I vaguely recalled from early school lessons about the "coureurs du bois" (the runners of the woods) and that French explorers had traversed what was at that time a very hostile land for Europeans. It still is, at minus forty degrees. At that number, Fahrenheit and Celsius are the same.

On this stretch of highway, we were seeing 'beware of elk' signs. The Zig was becoming quite skeptical about the odds of seeing any more wildlife in Canada, but I told him he was judging too soon. From the black silhouette on the metal sign, the elk looked like a bigger animal than the moose, with no leaping like the depiction of the deer. Who knows whether that's accurate; the answer would have to wait until I felt like playing with the computer search bar again.

Poplar fluff was blowing, and I was reminded that Manitoba, like many spots in many regions of the world, can be challenging for allergy sufferers. We put the top up and headed west.

Last words on weather? When I was a kid here I thought it was very humid in the summer. I remember that sweaty feeling and being so thrilled when a really good rainstorm rolled through in August. But now that I've lived in Georgia and spent a lot of time in Florida? You don't know 'humid' in Manitoba.

But you do know 'cold'. And 'flat'. Just like they do next door.

Some famous people born in, educated in, housed or claimed by Manitoba?
Businessman Izzy Asper. TV host Ashleigh Banfield. Cancer research activist and Canadian icon Terry Fox. Singer Oscar Brand. Actress Nia Vardalos. Author Carol Shields. Actor Will Arnett. Musician Tom Cochrane.

What to see next time?
The north. Riding Mountain National Park. Churchill and the polar bears. Gimli, with its energetic population of Scandinavian descendants. Flin Flon, which has to have one of the best place names in the country.

What to see more of?
The Canadian Museum of Human Rights.

What to see less of?
Winnipeg potholes. I saw and felt quite a few on this trip, but the Winnipeg brand seems to be a particularly distinctive one.

Surprises?
That the highway and the city roads were in such bad repair. It's a matter of opinion, of course, but I thought they were the worst in the country, worse than in Newfoundland or Nova Scotia where, arguably, they have fewer financial resources for highway construction and

weather that is just as hard on asphalt.

I know I'm harping on road conditions in almost every province. It's not that I'm running out of subjects to explore. For a road trip, this is a primary topic.

The Winnipeg roads were the unpleasant surprise. The pleasant surprise was the Museum of Human Rights. I had heard from others, since it opened in 2014, that it was a sight not to miss and they were right.

Chapter Eight

SASKATCHEWAN

Land of Living Skies

On a sunny day, Saskatchewan is an ocean, reversed: a sea of gold against a big, blue, unending sky. The wheat fields fill the eyes and eventually, the stomachs. Farming sustains the people here, and when you first see Saskatchewan, your overwhelming impression is of the land.

I think it's a place of great and timeless beauty.

The first town I saw after crossing the border from Manitoba into Saskatchewan, about twenty kilometers west of the Manitoba border, was called Moosomin. The city of Moose Jaw was a little farther on down the road. This sounded promising. Maybe I would clock my second moose sighting for this cross-Canada trip!

Moosomin was founded with the arrival of the Canadian Pacific Railway in the 1880s and it has a total population of about 2,500 people, the Zig read to me from his phone. The Trans-Canada was twinned through this area about eight years ago, and there's been a bit of a boom since, with signs of new hotel construction, residential land development, and increased natural resources activity—oil, potash, and wind energy.

Sights of the future and sights of the past. I saw a grain elevator, too, a reminder that Saskatchewan was, and still is, all about agriculture. On my previous drives across the country and across this province, grain elevators were once as numerous as gopher holes. They were the magnet of a town, the place where the work and efforts of hundreds, sometimes thousands, of people and families fused in a wooden tower with a great, living pile of seeds, drawn upward to a chute that sent them forth in a tidal wave of future food, a cascade pouring into a railway car heading for the coast and freighter transport across the ocean.

Now there's a vivid portrayal of the wheat pool. I doubt that many Saskatchewan farmers would describe it quite that way.

I always wondered what the reason was for calling them grain 'elevators', and I took advantage of the Zig's good nature and his ever-ready phone to have him look it up. Apparently, the grain elevator is built around an actual elevator, a system for moving the grain around while storing or transporting it. At one time, up until the 1990s, some prosperous communities had more than one, and many had an "elevator row" constructed in response to the demand created by so much production. As commodity prices fell, so did the need for so many wooden grain elevators, and now there is only one elevator row left in Canada, in Manitoba. Some single grain elevators are being preserved as museums or historic sites, in the prairie provinces, in B.C., and one in Ontario at Scugog (the oldest in Canada and second oldest in the Americas).

It is so cool to be able to look all this up and continue moving across the landscape at the same time. In the PreSearchBar Days, gathering information like that would have required a trip to a library at the very least.

The landscape is so flat here, too, that you can put the car on cruise control and allow your mind to wander up and down the lists you've concocted. Famous people from Saskatchewan, like singer Joni Mitchell and actor Boris Karloff. Place names about animals, like Duck Lake, Oxbow, and Turtleford. And things that make Saskatchewan unique, which includes producing more hockey players per capita than any other province and refusing to turn the clock back and forward in fall and spring, as do the other provinces. Geographically, it's located in the Mountain Time Zone but it observes Central

Time, as does Manitoba, and doesn't change twice a year because . . . well, it's not clear why. I remember hearing a story when I was a kid that it was because Daylight Saving Time upset the cows and messed up their biological clocks when it came to milking time.

Setting the time is within provincial jurisdiction in Canada, and each province decides its own. Saskatchewan is in the same time zone as Alberta, in the Mountain Time Zone, for six months of the year, and matches Manitoba for the other six months. Is that a case of not going on Daylight Saving Time? Or being on Daylight Saving Time all the time? Depends which time zone you're standing in when you answer the question.

Okay, I've thoroughly bored myself, and perhaps you also.

Outside the car windows, the fields still looked much the same and the sky was still absolutely huge. Wind farms were spread out over almost every ridge. The roads were really good, no potholes or endless construction zones to contend with. Besides moose, it's possible to spot deer, elk, and caribou—maybe much more likely, given the wide open spaces, than in the heavily forested Atlantic provinces.

I had been to and through Saskatchewan many times. If you dropped me into the center of a wheat field, I think I would know, from the topography of the land and the nature of the sky, that I was in Saskatchewan and not in Manitoba or Alberta. And yet, even though it was so familiar, it felt new on this trip, maybe because I was different. I wanted to see and smell and feel everything as if it were new. Bill Bryson wrote that "to my mind, the greatest reward and luxury of travel is to be able to experience everyday things as if for the first time, to be in a position in which almost nothing is so familiar it is taken for granted."

On this trip, I had decided to use the Trans-Canada Highway as much as possible and so was headed into Regina, the capital city. I've been to Saskatoon, Saskatchewan's other major city, many times. Regina, I did not know as well. As I drove though the outskirts of town, I was impressed with the diversity, with numerous

Korean, Vietnamese, Greek, and other restaurants to be seen, and the word "African" on many signs and doorways. Cuisine in Saskatchewan, as in most corners of Canada, had become interesting and diverse. Time was when all you could get in the prairie provinces was steak or hamburger, mashed potatoes, pierogis, and beer. Now, it seemed that ethnic dishes, recipes based on meals prepared by the indigenous people before the Europeans arrived, and variations on the old farmhouse standards were easy to find.

On previous trips, I had been introduced to Saskatoon berry jam, pies, and chutney, and I was looking forward to a repeat experience.

I was impressed with the very organized look of Regina. Lovely parks near the Wascana Parkway featured paved walking paths, and I could see many frail elderly people out getting their exercise in the fresh air. That's not so easy in winter, but in August it was beautiful.

The climate in Saskatchewan is not for the nervous. You have to make up your mind just to get out and about, no matter what the temperature or the wind chill factor. That's not to say that nobody thinks about it or talks about it; sometimes, it seems like it's all anybody talks about. (That's not a characteristic unique to Saskatchewan, by the way.)

But talking is one thing and doing is another. People in Saskatchewan don't huddle inside when it's cold. They get out and enjoy the cold, the snow, and the ice. They cut holes in it and pull fish out. They skate, they ski, they ride snowmobiles. The vehicles are all geared to the climate, and if you end up in a snow bank, you just rock it out or get towed. You do the things you should to prevent your engine or your gas line from freezing up. If your battery dies, you get a jump (and it is never hard to get help in Saskatchewan). You might want to ask for a "boost", though, just to make sure the Canadian knows what you mean. You'll notice as you drive around the towns and cities that there are posts with electrical outlets in them. When you go out in winter, even just to a store for half an hour, you plug in the block heater of your car so that it will start when you come out.

The wind is another significant figure in the Saskatchewan weather picture. When you don't have many hills in the way, that sucker can come sweeping across the landscape like a freight train with a braking problem.

The tradeoff for the crisp temperatures is the clear sky. Sunshine pours through, all winter long (except when there's a blizzard).

In the summer, temperatures can be equally noteworthy, in the other direction. It can be really hot, although we weren't seeing any of that extreme on the particular August days we were there. The highest recorded temperature in Saskatchewan was 45° C (113° F) in Yellow Grass in 1937. In 2012, the CBC was reporting record temperatures broken in July, with the highest in Maple Creek at 34.9° C (94.8° F) and again this year, in June, with Moose Jaw, Regina, and many other places setting records.

The lowest temperature ever recorded in the province was -47.8°F in Swift Current one February day in 1936. It's that .8° that really gets you.

Our plan for Regina was to check in at the Hotel Saskatchewan downtown, one of the chain of Canadian Pacific Railway hotels mostly built in the early twentieth century. These CP Hotels showcased the best design, materials, and spare-no-expense frill that the money of the day could buy. They tended to sit on prime real estate, often river or harbor front, and resembled the sort of castles that might command the views of a European river and occupy the top of the list of items that a baron or an earl was handing down to an heir. As a result, in the biggest Canadian cities, the price for a night at a CP Hotel was somewhat stiff. In Regina, though, it was quite reasonable and after a few nights in places providing a less than perfect sleep, I decided to treat myself to more luxurious digs.

The very first CP hotels in Canada were built even earlier, in the mid 1880s, some of them in major cities near the railway depot to accommodate railway passengers and some of them in rural areas, built either to provide a majestic, mountain experience or to provide a stopping place to get a meal in the days before the use of dining cars on a train became widespread.

We strolled up to the front desk through a lobby decorated like a nineteenth-century opera house or museum. High ceilings, wide hallways, paintings, mirrors, thick carpeting, and historical photographs made us feel very elegant, and I was regretting not bringing the ball gown. Not that I was badly dressed, just somewhere in the middle, and a little wrinkled after sitting in the car all day. I caught sight of my hair in one of the mirrors and was reminded that I was riding around in a convertible. But no one at the front desk batted an eye or made a comment. Years ago, I did a radio interview with the owner of a school for international diplomats who said that's the classic definition of good manners: when you can make everyone around you feel comfortable and completely lacking in self-consciousness or self-criticism.

At some of the places we've been, I could tell that I was just one in a long line of guests or visitors. At this hotel, by contrast, the people at the desk made a fuss over us.

"Welcome to Regina," the young man said.

"Thank you," I replied. "We've come all the way from Georgia."

"Well, we know that," he said. "We saw your reservation. Then we saw you drive up to the door and we saw your U.S. plates. We'd be excited about somebody from next door in Montana but all the way from Georgia? Wow."

Canadians are nice.

"We're upgrading you," he added. "We're putting you in the Premier's Suite."

Well, la di da. This was getting even better.

"What if he shows up and wants his room?" Zig asked. Funny man.

The young reception clerk grinned back at him. "We'll be alright."

The next morning we heard that the Premier *had* been in the hotel that night. They put him in the Royal Suite.

Royalty has stayed here many times, I learned from a plaque on the downtown pedestrian mall. The Queen and the Duke of Edinburgh in 2005. Prince Charles in 2001 and 2012. Princess Anne in 2004 and 2007. Prince Edward visited in 2003, 2006, and in 2014. And those are just the trips in this century.

I started to think back on all the places we'd stopped or passed that had a royal reference (the Crown and Moose pub in Corner Brook Newfoundland; Annapolis Royal in Nova Scotia; Mount Royal in Montréal Québec; Kingston Ontario—not to mention all the Princes, Albert, George, etc.) They came up many times in the places I planned to see, too—the Royal Tyrrell Museum near Drumheller, Alberta; Victoria, B.C., named for Queen Victoria; and Regina itself, using the Latin word for queen.

All these identifiers were a reminder of the historical influence of the British Empire and its stress on kings, queens, princes, and princesses in the sixteenth to nineteenth centuries when these places were being renamed. You see it through the States, too—we have lots of Charlottes, Georgetowns, and state names with royal histories (Georgia, Maryland, the Carolinas), although we don't have a Queen on the money, the way we do in Canada. Queen Elizabeth the Second is head of state and Canada is a member of the British Commonwealth, although those are ceremonial ties now, rather than having any active meaning in today's daily activities or exercise of power.

We walked around Regina for about an hour. The city was clean and interesting, although it's not a shopping mecca or a place to find musicians busking on the street. At least, it wasn't on the day we were there.

We walked over to Victoria Park, across the street from the hotel. It was 4 p.m. on a summer Sunday, and the park—with its open spaces, grass, and trees—was warm, sunny, and inviting. But almost no one was there. The pedestrian mall was almost deserted too. It might have been that there wasn't enough residential downtown citythrob to generate energy for the shopping areas, although there had, apparently, been some new development of warehouses into condos and lofts in Regina. It also might just have been my perspective and my basis for comparison. After three years in the U.S., even spending a lot of time in less populated areas, many Canadian places seemed rather empty to me.

We decided to try out the food in the hotel and sat down in the lounge because the restaurant, having done a big Sunday brunch that we just missed, was closed until breakfast the next morning. On the recommendation of the server (who, on hearing about our epic road trip, shared that she and her family were into fast-paced road trips, too, and often drove from Regina to Nova Scotia in a couple of days), we ordered a nice local draught beer, made from lentils, and an excellent pasta (pappardelle with shaved parmesan).

I hadn't seen much while walking around to entice me back out in the evening, and it was Sunday after all. Maybe if it had been Saturday night or an evening in winter, with a Regina Pats hockey game going on at the Brandt Arena, I would have been on a quest for live entertainment, but tonight seemed just fine in front of the TV set.

Hockey is the sport in Saskatchewan, as it is everywhere in the country. It is Canada's game, and many (if not most) kids back in the day either played on teams or in casual games of street hockey, called 'shinny' in these parts, in their neighborhoods on winter days after school. It's become a lot more expensive as the years have gone by, though, and a lot of families turn to indoor soccer or basketball for a team sport for their kids these days.

I didn't ever play hockey myself but I knew a lot of hockey players and watched a lot of games. In the States you can see it live or on TV anywhere now, although there isn't nearly the intensity of interest, of course, as there is in football. You wouldn't pick hockey as a small-talk topic the way you would football, in certain circles.

For myself, I was not one of those relocated Canadians who immediately went looking, on arrival in America, for the nearest ice rink. If somebody offered me playoff tickets and there weren't higher priorities that night, I'd go. If that shocks and appalls you, maybe you should let me know and if I get any hockey tickets, I'll pass them on to you.

When winter comes, people pull out the skates and the ice-fishing gear. In the summer, it is baseball gloves or hiking boots. For spectator sports, it's football in the fall and hockey in the winter, and hockey playoffs in the spring.

We were deep into a movie when there was a knock at the door, and I opened it to a server carrying a dessert plate on a lovely tray. In the midst of strawberries, blueberries, and melon, someone had written in melted chocolate "Best Road Trip Ever."

The Canadians at this hotel were extra-nice.

The next morning, we had breakfast in the dining room, with its high ceilings, velvet wing chairs, fireplaces, and hot buffet. We were greeted by the hotel manager, a man from Senegal who had worked all over Europe, in Memphis for two years, the Yukon territory for three years, and now five years in Regina. He was extremely enthusiastic about Yukon and told us about his favorite spot, Emerald Lake, as well as the many moose he'd seen during his stay in Yellowknife. Maybe I'll have to go there soon.

We retrieved the car from the parking lot and headed west. The next driving leg took us toward Moose Jaw. As I mentioned earlier, I had decided to stick with the Trans-Canada Highway through Saskatchewan, although that removed Saskatoon, one of the two other major cities in the province (Prince Albert is the third), from the route. It was not an easy decision, because we had already made a few digressions from Highway 1 and we could have done that now. I had visited family in Saskatoon many times over the years and, since our itinerary included Red Deer, in central Alberta to the west, I could have drawn the line going north from Regina to Saskatoon and then over to Alberta. The Guess Who's song "Running Back to Saskatoon" and Burton Cumming's voice were running through my mind, and I almost made the change. Saskatoon and the North Saskatchewan river valley are lovely in the summer.

But I wanted to see the rest of southern Saskatchewan, and so we rolled on westward. The experience of this highway is almost meditative, and I was so deep into my own thoughts and inner images that I was startled when billboards announced to me that we were near the Tunnels of Moose Jaw, a tourist attraction where we could explore the story of Chicago gangster Al Capone's visits to the city in the 1920s or learn about the lives of early Chinese immigrants. Sounded intriguing, but maybe next time.

We also decided to take a pass on visiting Gravelbourg, "a touch of Europe on the Prairies". Even though the billboard was enticing, we decided to stay on course.

Through this area, you see more of the huge open fields. The land is so flat you can see for ten miles or more. The color is golden, the sky so big, and the weather so gentle. Signs were there, though, that fall wasn't far off. The leaves were beginning to turn color, even though it was only August. The grass around the small ponds of water on the farms along the highway was going brown and dormant, but there wasn't any ice on those sloughs yet. That has been known to happen in August, though.

One of my favorite authors for capturing the Saskatchewan spirit is W.O. Mitchell Others are Sharon Butala, Max Braithwaite, Allan Fotheringham, and Guy Vanderhaege.

Looking at the wheat fields, I started flashing back to my Grade 3 (In the U.S., third grade—in Canada, Grade 3) art project experience, remembering my lifelong conclusion that I was "bad at art". The teacher had asked us to find materials at home that could be used to create a collage that we would make by sketching a picture and then filling in the colors by cutting and pasting these materials onto a thin piece of board. I was eager and got inspired, like you do at that age. I decided to do a scene of a farm at sunrise, with a train rolling by. I collected a small red rock to be the rising sun, black pipe cleaners to be the silhouette of the train, and dozens of pieces of uncooked spaghetti pasta to be the wheat fields in the foreground.

I was a more than a little intimidated when I saw the beads, fabric pieces, bits of gold braid, carefully dyed leather, sequins, glitter, and feathers some of the other kids had used for their projects. I had taken the "materials you have at home" instruction very literally, and I don't think the others did (although maybe sequins and feathers were a usual item in some sixties-era homes?). The subjects chosen were quite different from mine too. We saw a lot of pictures of dolls and cowboys. No other landscapes. I didn't get the 10 out of 10 or the gold star. I forget exactly what mark she gave me, but it was low. I remember the picture very clearly though, and all that spaghetti, lined up just so.

That was the end of my artistic career, but not of my fascination with the Saskatchewan countryside. A few of the artists who've done far better in portraying it are Sharon Marshall, Kathy Bradshaw, Paul Constable, Dan Reid, and Mary Longman.

Landscape, of course, is not the only way of expressing Saskatchewan. One of the most famous of Saskatchewan artists is sculptor Joe Fafard, whose work focuses on animals and people. Music and language also portray the land, preserve some of the past and give expression to the people's feeling for their province.

The imagery of indigenous culture and First Nations language and experience are woven through Saskatchewan art and literature. One of the Cree languages is the source of the name Saskatchewan, which translates as 'swiftly flowing river'. The names given many of the towns in Saskatchewan were intriguing, too. Moose Jaw, in south-central Saskatchewan, is about seventy-five klicks west of Regina. The Zig looked it up on his phone as we traveled and found a couple of theories on the origin of the name: that it comes from the shape of the river through the area where the city developed, or that it came from the Plains Cree word moose gaw, meaning 'warm breezes', which are a result of the geographic protection offered to the river valley by the nearby mountain range.

Moose Jaw is also home to the Snowbirds, the Canadian Forces airshow demonstration team.

I remembered hearing some eminent author on Morningside talking to Peter Gzowski about the emotional attachment that Canadians do or do not have toward their country. He suggested that the patriotism here is different, in kind, to that of the neighbors to the south or of Europeans. It's not that Canadians love their country any less, it's that they don't speak of it or celebrate it as loudly as is done elsewhere.

He also suggested that perhaps it was because people

do so much traveling nowadays that they don't become enamored of, or perhaps ensnared by (my words, not his), a place as they do when they spend more time immobile.

I'm not sure that follows, logically or necessarily. It seems to me that traveling could be exactly the activity that leads to a deep and binding affection for a place. The more traveling you do, the more you love your own place when you return. That was my experience, anyway.

Peter Gzowski is one of the famous Canadians claimed by Saskatchewan because he lived in Moose Jaw for one year, as a young journalist in the fifties. The final broadcast of his national, Toronto-based radio programme Morningside was done from Moose Jaw. I worked with him, as a contributor from Vancouver, and occasionally interviewed him for our show *The Early Edition*, when he was passing through town talking about a new book or the golf tournament that he headlined each year to raise money for literacy. He was always amiable and happy to see us in Vancouver, telling me once that he always looked forward to coming to our studio because no one told him he couldn't smoke there. He smoked a lot—one report was that it was as many as eighty cigarettes a day. Sadly, he died of emphysema in 2002.

Another 170 kilometers west of Moose Jaw, we arrived at Swift Current, Saskatchewan, also known as Speedy Creek. Its motto is "where life makes sense". I love the implication by omission here, that there are many other places where life does not make sense.

Come to think of it, I think I've been to those places.

The view of boundless fields of wheat, waving in a gentle breeze, continued to roll past my window. Saskatchewan farmland might have been in my history, if my forebears had stopped on their westward trek instead of pushing on to Alberta. But they did, and the next province has family, friends, and career memories on the horizon.

One more of the Canadian prairie provinces to go. "Texas of the North" was in my windshield now.

Other famous people born in, educated in, housed or

claimed by Saskatchewan?
Singer/songwriter/artist Joni Mitchell. Actor Boris Karloff. Author Joy Kogawa. Actor Leslie Nielsen. Hockey coach Mike Babcock. Hockey player Gordie Howe. Author Farley Mowat. TV host Art Linkletter.

What to see next time?
Saskatoon. The northern part of the province.

What to see more of?
Jars of Saskatoon berries, lining the trunk of my car.

What to see less of?
Speed limit signs. On a vast, flat plain like this, you could safely drive a lot faster than the signs say, I think. You come across very few twists and turns, visibility goes on and on, and compared to other places, traffic is light. Why not raise the limit—even have no speed limit, as they do on the Autobahn in Germany and in some other parts of Europe? Now, this might have to be amended, somewhat, based on time of year and road conditions in winter, but why not? In the summer months, allow drivers to choose their own speed while driving across the hundreds of flat miles in Saskatchewan? Might be quite a tourist draw.

Surprises?
The absence of people on the streets in Regina, although seeing it only on a Sunday may be quite a limited perspective.

Chapter Nine

ALBERTA

Is Alberta Canada's Texas, or is Texas the American Alberta?

Alberta and Texas do have a lot in common. Both have economies tied to oil, agriculture, and cattle ranching. Both have communities that revolve around rodeo. But while Texas has a coastline and a border shared with Mexico, Alberta has mountains and blizzards. And hockey.

The Trans-Canada Highway guided me into Medicine Hat after crossing the border from Saskatchewan to Alberta. This is a fairly large city on the South Saskatchewan River and most Albertans refer to it as 'the Hat'. Cuddled by a gently sloping valley, it was a gathering place for the Cree, the Blackfoot, and the Assiniboine people for many years before Europeans arrived. The name came from the English translation of "saamis", a Blackfoot word for the eagle tail feather headdress worn by a medicine man or woman.

The landscape from Saskatchewan into Alberta didn't change much. The golden wheat fields, the endless sky, and the straight, flat highway all added to the almost hypnotic power of the prairie countryside. I saw Medicine Hat coming for many miles before we actually drove into it.

A few hundred miles ago, I pondered the unusual place names I was seeing along the way. One of the quirkiest is Head-Smashed-In Buffalo Jump, Alberta, named for the hunting methods of the ancient indigenous people who drove the buffalo into a frenzy, chased them toward a cliff, and then harvested them after they'd stampeded over. This UNESCO World Heritage site is on Highway 785, a little off the beaten track of the Trans-Canada, eighteen kilometers northwest of Fort Macleod. You might think the smashed-in head referred to the outcome for the unfortunate buffalo, but the legend goes that the place was named for a Blackfoot warrior who wanted to see the hunt from a spot below the cliff and then was killed when his skull was crushed by the falling animals. The risks of changing perspective.

Now, I don't mean to imply that the prairie provinces have the strangest names in the country. After all, I saw Placentia, Dildo, and Conception Bay in Newfoundland and Labrador. Mushaboom in Nova Scotia. Saint-Louis-du-Ha!Ha! in Québec. Punkeydoodles Corners and Wawa in Ontario. Spuzzum and Skookumchuk in British Columbia. But the prairie provinces do have some good ones: Flin Flon, Manitoba. Mosquito Grizzly Bears Head Lean Man, Saskatchewan (actually, the combination of three aboriginal tribes in 1898 rather than a summary of a three-act play or a hippie's description of a wild game entrée recipe). And Dead Man's Flats, Alberta. Fort Qu'Appelle, Saskatchewan. Vulcan, Alberta. Passamaquoddy Bay, Manitoba.

In the Hat that Tuesday, it was warm for August. I stopped at a mall to pick up some popcorn, granola bars, water, and protein shakes for the road. The mall interior was strung with Canadian flags and Canada 150 signage.

We finished the so-called road lunch and knew there had to be more than this. Medicine Hat has the same chain fast-food restaurants as any other place, but you can find some really interesting Alberta-specific cuisine there and all across the province: grilled beef steak with rosemary; wild game dishes with bison, wild boar, or elk; Taber corn, cabbage rolls, and pierogis. Stop at a deli or food store and pick up some Alberta mustard, Grizzly gouda cheese, or canola oil. If we were in Calgary at Stampede time (that's the annual exhibition, fair, and rodeo in July), we'd have a pancake breakfast.

And if you want to consume something and tip your hat to history at the same time, the Bloody Caesar cocktail was invented by a Calgary bartender in 1969.

We decided to take back roads for a while and turned off on Highway 56. The Zig loves to drive and, while he appreciated the efficiency of getting from point A to point B quickly and bought in to the overall goal of driving the Trans-Canada, he had been lobbying for a slow road for some time, and I wanted to be cooperative.

There was much less traffic on this two-lane highway and my convertible was the only vehicle for miles. The landscape was somehow restful and serene, with the acres and acres of golden then sandy-colored fields and just an occasional tree. I saw sloughs of blue water, a deeper blue even than the huge sky. Windmills commanded the ridges.

Almost by design rather than coincidence, the next song that came over the speakers was a classic from Ian Tyson, one of Canada's legendary musicians. Alberta music has everything from folk to rock to classical to jazz to country in the spotlight. I've mentioned quite a few musicians from other provinces and in Alberta the list is equally interesting. Chad Kroeger from the group Nickelback (where, the story goes, when they were working in a coffee shop in Hanna, Alberta, they named the band after the constant question asked of customers who paid with paper money, "do you want your nickel back?"). k.d. lang. Paul Brandt. Jann Arden.

As we went north, the landscape wasn't quite as flat, and I started to see rolling hills. The next highlight was to be Drumheller, the city that is home to the Royal Terrell Museum, at the edge of the Badlands. Again, an intriguing name. It's a generic, descriptive word 'badlands', and you'll find them all over the world, in Argentina, Italy, Taiwan, the U.S., Spain, and New Zealand. Some of the sources I looked up credited the Lakota people in the U.S. with the name 'mako sica', which translates as 'land bad'. French-Canadian fur trappers called it 'les mauvais terres', apparently. In Spanish, it was 'malpais'. You'll see steep hills and cliffs, very little vegetation or water.

The landscape was a mesmerizing scene of hoodoos (tall, thin spikes of rock) and coulees (valleys formed millennia ago through the erosion caused by streams long since dried up). If you are familiar with Canadian Tom Cochrane's video of the song "Life is a Highway", covered by Rascal Flatts for the movie *Cars*, you've seen the hoodoos and the Canadian Badlands. It's a brilliant video.) We had been rolling along through wheat fields and farmland, and then that all changed dramatically and quickly when we left the Trans-Canada Highway to head toward the center of the province to visit family in Red Deer and to stop in the city of Drumheller, just a few miles from the internationally famous Royal Tyrrell Museum. I've visited this museum a few other times and didn't plan to make a stop this time, but if you're following along in this book, this is one adaptation of your own that I would urge you to make. It's a center of paleontological research (there's a double on the American/Canadian spelling differences, with the 'er' vs. 're' in center, and a 'paleon' vs. 'palaeon' on the word about the study of fossil animals and plants).

The museum features many galleries depicting the astounding scientific discoveries in the study of dinosaurs over the decades of this century, with an emphasis on the significance of the Alberta Badlands and the ancient fossil finds here.

You could also consider a detour to UNESCO World Heritage Site Dinosaur Provincial Park, located about 175 kilometers to the southeast and a magnet for those who want an outdoors, camping, and hiking experience along with their exposure to new information.

The fossils that lie all around this region, where active archaeological digs are still underway, are the spine of the Alberta story, the oil that's provided its prosperity, its 'boom and bust' reality, and the controversy over the way we all use the natural resources of the planet. Makes for great debates around the campfire after you've actually spent a day on the scene of something, rather than getting your facts from Twitter, TV, or books.

After driving through the Badlands, we emerged into a landscape that changed back to grain fields almost instantly. It was a swift and startling transition, much like the one between the western edge of the Canadian Shield in northern Ontario and the beginning of the prairie in Manitoba or the one between the Alberta wheat fields and the foothills, with the wall of mountain to be seen beyond. We passed two herds of bison and, at one point, I thought I saw a fox zip by. I was staying on alert for a beaver sighting and possibly a Rocky Mountain goat, a few hundred klicks farther to the west and a few thousand feet higher above sea level. Also for a moose, although I wasn't betting the farm on it.

While riding along, I shut down the MP3 player and started hitting the radio buttons. The local station, in Consort, Alberta, was leading the sports report with the chuckwagon racing results. Rodeo is big in Alberta. So is hockey. After that, I'd group football, skiing, snowboarding, and curling, with figure skating and basketball not far behind. If you are from Alberta and you disagree, you could write your own book.

We had decided to bypass Calgary this time but would reconnect with the Trans-Canada after doing part of the Banff-Jasper Highway through the Rockies. I went out to Alberta to take a television reporting job in Edmonton in the seventies, and I was also in Calgary quite a bit at that time. Edmonton, the provincial capital, was the politics and government city, Calgary was the business city, although of course they each had some of both. Calgary was where many of the American multinationals located their Canadian head offices, if they weren't going to use Toronto. Edmonton was where the cabinet ministers and members of the legislative assembly ran the province. Both were the setting for the hundreds of press conferences, media announcements, and photo ops that I covered.

I remember meeting Prime Minister Pierre Trudeau for the first time in Calgary in the late seventies. I would have to say he's one of the most intelligent people I ever had the opportunity to interview. Not the most memorable though: that interview came in the eighties when I hosted the Vancouver CBC Radio morning show *The Early Edition* and had the opportunity to speak with Bishop Desmond Tutu of South Africa, winner of the Nobel Prize for Peace in 1984. The most down-to-earth was Wayne Gretzky, a calm, unpretentious man even though, at only nineteen years old, he'd just been named 'most valuable player' in his sport. The funniest was novelist Max Braithwaite.

I won't mention the ones I remember with unhappy associations. Life's too short.

The highlight, I'd have to say, was meeting the Queen and Prince Philip in Edmonton. It was at a reception for reporters who covered her tour for the Commonwealth Games in 1978 and mostly what I recall was the (large!) number of rules and protocol guidelines we had to follow. Curtsy when you meet her. Once you get into the reception room, stand in one place—don't circulate, they will move around the room and come to you. Don't touch her. If she extends a hand to you, take it politely. Don't grab it, don't shake it enthusiastically, don't hurt her. Don't speak to her unless she speaks to you.

It was the late afternoon of the day that the Royal Tour had taken them outside Edmonton to the small town of Vegreville, the center of much of the heritage preservation of Alberta's Ukrainian immigrants. A large Ukrainian Easter egg had been put up outside town about three years earlier and, at that time, it was the largest in the world. Thirty-one feet long, three-and-a-half stories high, and about 2,300 kilograms, more than 5,000 pounds. This pysanka was set at a thirty-degree angle to the ground and was built to turn with the wind, like a weather vane. (The engineering and computer science aspects of building it are quite fascinating, and I send you to the Search Bar.)

When the Queen and Prince Philip approached our small group of reporters, she smiled at us and commented on the horses and riders they'd seen in Calgary a couple of days earlier. Someone asked if she had enjoyed the chuckwagon race demonstration, and she said yes, but that she had had to warn Prince Philip that they wouldn't be trying any of that back at home. Someone asked them about their impressions of the events around Edmonton that day, and Prince Philip commented that for him the highlight was the Easter Egg near Vegreville. I said (trying to be helpful and informative) that the egg was very authentic, and he replied that that must have been a challenge for the chicken. He said it in a very elegant, reserved way, and it wasn't until my drive home, I remember, once the nerves were back under control, that I got the joke.

Driving north toward Red Deer, the day was very warm (although not quite as seriously hot as I've been used to in Georgia). The Alberta climate is very similar to Saskatchewan's, although not quite as cold in winter. The air quality was noticeably crummier than I remembered from previous stays in the province, and that was because of the forest fire situation in B.C.'s interior that August.

It was shaping up to be one of the worst years ever, breaking records that had been in place for nearly sixty years. The winds were taking the smoke a long way east into Alberta, and west to the coast, into the densely populated Lower Mainland around Vancouver. From time to time, I could smell it even in Red Deer. The B.C. government had declared a state of emergency, and thousands of people had been evacuated. We had some reservations about driving toward it rather than south, or even east, back the way we came, but in the end we just decided to keep an eye on the many sources of information about the day-to-day developments and push onward.

After an enjoyable hike in Red Deer, over a bridge where a moose once was, we left the city the next day at 6 a.m., heading west on Highway 11 toward Rocky Mountain House. As the western sky started to glow pink from the sunrise, we stopped for breakfast at the Shell/A&W in Rocky, where the fresh-baked muffins were divine. Then on to Nordegg, where the foothills and the mountains were coming into sight. At Abraham Lake (watch for it on the left, if you are reading this and trying to follow along) we stopped to look at the turquoise blue water and take photographs.

The tops of the range of mountains looked so old— ancient rock against a crystal clear blue sky. Then just past David Thompson Resort, the mountains turned misty, resembling a Japanese painting. It was the smoke from the wild fires in the British Columbia interior. The mountains got darker and so did the sky; it seemed like twilight, at eight in the morning. My nose was tickling, my eyes were itching.

We drove straight toward a mountain with red and

gold horizontal stripes that looked close enough to touch. Then the road curved, and I was looking at a craggy peak with a white collar. An ice field. The smoke lifted somewhat and the view was amazing.

When you're on Highway 93 (also called the Banff-Jasper Highway and The Icefields Parkway), there are mountains on all three sides—four, if you look in the rearview mirror. Fires had gone through on the north side of the road, this year and in years gone by. The trees were just trunks, with leaves blown or burned off. Some of the trees were lying on the hillside, some stood alone, bare and blackened.

We were about three hours from Red Deer now. The smoke had lifted a bit, but my throat was still scratchy and I was coughing. I could see virtually no other cars on this road. Then we entered Banff National Park, where a sign informed us that it is unlawful to feed wildlife.

I have come through Banff and Jasper National Parks in other years and encountered a long line of cars parked on the shoulder. It was a sign that someone had spotted a Rocky Mountain goat, an elk, a moose, or even a bear, and everyone had their cameras out. I guess some foolish ones even throw food toward these wild animals.

We approached the park gate, where you usually have to buy a park pass. Because of the 150th birthday, this year was the exception, and entrance to all the national parks was free.

All along the Icefields Parkway, I saw majestic mountains and glaciers hanging off the rock. This was the southern half of Highway 93, and it seemed there were fewer vehicles going from Jasper south to Banff than the other way around.

We pulled off the road at Bow Valley summit, a popular hiking trail, hoping for a photo opportunity. You can't see much from the parking lot though, so then the discussion was—do we want to stop for a hike? What would that do to our plan to get to Vancouver by tonight? Would it be any fun anyway with all the smoke in the air? A few dozen other people were climbing out of their cars and pulling on their backpacks; clearly, they'd made the call 'in favor', but the road west won out, and we pulled back onto the highway.

At the junction of Highway 93 and Highway 1, just before we were about to head out of Alberta and toward the pass into B.C., I decided to go into Lake Louise. Lake Louise is one of the most famous spots in the Rockies, the location of a charming alpine town and a killer ski resort. All of a sudden, we went from a mildly busy highway to a traffic jam, right in the middle of the Canadian wilderness. Cars, trucks, and RVs were bumper to fender in a line snaking toward the village and off as far as the eye could see. We went past the village up to Moraine Lake. The parking lot was full, and there were people directing traffic. I have been to the lake before so decided to pass on it this time, just because of the crowds. But if you've never seen it, it's definitely worth a stop. I'm not saying 'don't go' just because of a few vehicles in your way—you have more determination than that, haven't you?

You take a short walk from the parking lot, and then there is the breathtaking, iconic view of the lake, the Chateau, and the Victoria Glacier. Someday, I'd like to see it as they did in the olden days, before there were sixty others there at the same time. Might have to go at midnight.

We had the top down on the convertible and could strongly smell the smoke in the air. But once we got back on the Trans-Canada, and were rolling along at the speed limit, the smoke drifted off and we could smell that clear, fresh mountain air. Not cold though. August in the Rockies, you're still doing summer.

I could see the railroad tracks alongside us, and I couldn't stop the "Canadian Railroad Trilogy" from playing in my mental soundtrack. The railroad story is Canada's story. Without it, provinces would not have joined Confederation; there would be no 'a Mari usque ad Mare' (Canada's motto, 'from sea to sea'.)

When I told people about this cross-Canada journey, many thought it sounded cool but said they would rather go by rail. Taking a train across Canada, that sounds like a unique, peak life experience.

Let me raise the bar. How about driving one? I'd pay big money for that—anybody would! Via Rail, are you listening?

On a previous trip, I took a look at Canmore and at Banff. Canmore was once a tiny village a few miles down the road from the National Park gates. In my memory, it was significant because of the time, back in the seventies, when a ski rack blew right off the top of the aged toy auto I was driving and had to be retrieved from the ditch some miles back. Canmore, like so many towns at the edge of ski runs, had quite a hippie vibe forty years ago. This day it looked like a mini Whistler or mini Park City or mini Aspen or any one of a dozen alpine villages. It was clean and pretty, but most of the funky side was gone—at least so it seemed to this traveler passing through.

It is the challenge (and the definition) of every travel writer that you are "just passing through." People become annoyed about what they perceive as your arrogance in presuming to evaluate their place or their lives, but I insist that what I am doing is just reacting, just giving my personal, unique reactions to a place based on my own experience, opinions, frame of mind, and intentions for the next leg of the journey. Yours will probably be very different—in fact they most definitely are. Nobody is right or wrong, just different.

All along the highway, a glimpse of wildlife was promised. Signs showing the shapes of deer, moose, elk, mountain goats, and bighorn sheep shared ironic space with signs announcing Alberta's anti-cellphone, distracted-driving law.

When I got to Banff, the people-watching made up for the lack of wildlife viewing. The contrast and diversity on Banff Avenue were intriguing: families, loving couples, guys with Harley vests, guys with cowboy hats, and goth women with plaid miniskirts, torn fishnet stockings, and spikes through their ears—three of them! Maybe they were a visiting girl singing group. I saw trendy men in shiny raspberry, mustard, and marmalade-colored jeans (one color per pair). But, yes, I also saw many serious hikers, wearing boots and backpacks.

When you first encounter the Rockies, the beauty takes your breath away. These majestic giants appear to have been there, towering over all, since the beginning of time. The contrast between the loveliness of the open, golden prairie and the splendor of the mountains is another, jaw-dropping aspect of the phenomenon that is Alberta. This is a wonderful, stunning place. Zig told me that I made almost the same comment about every one of the nine Canadian provinces so far, and that reminded me of Emerson's observation that "though we travel the world over to find the beautiful, we must carry it with us or we find it not."

Alberta is a boom-or-bust place, its fortunes tied to the price of oil, just like Texas. All of the Canadian provinces, in one way or another, have their economies tied to their natural resources; I can't remember when I first heard, was told, or read that 'Canada is a hewer of wood and a drawer of water' but I do know it was the first of dozens, if not hundreds of times. Alberta's neighbor to the west is also a creature of its natural resources. This is just one thing they have in common: economic realities, urban/rural patterns, orientation south rather than east. What they do not have in common? Weather, water (salt and ocean versus fresh, lakes and rivers) and degree of connection to other Pacific Rim regions. The Rocky Mountains are often seen as a barrier, a divider between the two provinces, despite the passes and the railroad. Where Alberta looks south, B.C. looks west.

Some famous people born in, educated in, housed or claimed by Alberta?
Actor Nathan Fillion. Singer Robert Goulet. Hockey players Wayne Gretzky, Mark Messier. Figure skater Jamie Salé. Actresses Elisha Cuthbert and Evangeline Lilly. Author Rudy Wiebe.

What to see next time?
Edmonton, with its beautiful river valley, the university where I studied for four full-time years and two part-time years.

Jasper, the other town in the Rockies. Very different from Banff. Driving toward Jasper from Edmonton, the approach is quite distinctive compared to driving toward Banff, from Calgary. The southern route, from Calgary, has the foothills coming into sight, nestled at the base of the mountains. The northern route, from Edmonton, has a wide, four-lane divided highway stretching out toward a typical prairie horizon, suddenly surrounded by a mountain range, filling your windshield.

What to see more of?
The Alberta cattle ranch experience. Maybe a trail ride.

The museums and the multicultural mosaic. The Easter Egg at Vegreville, again.

What to see less of?
The overcrowded, well-advertised places that thousands of tourists have put on their 'bucket lists'. Lake Louise, the towns of Banff and Jasper, the Bow River are all stupendous to see, there is no argument. But if you've seen them already, do yourself and other people who are seeing them for the first (and perhaps the only) time a favor and stay away. Leave some room for other people.

Surprises?
Not many, after being born in Alberta, living there nine years as a child, then four years as a young working adult. But that was back in the eighties—what did I see, new, this time? And what was surprising? The cosmopolitan atmosphere everywhere. Asian stores, restaurants, signs.

That there wasn't more construction work in the national parks than there was, given what I saw in other provinces.

No wildlife.

Chapter Ten

BRITISH COLUMBIA

The mountains are calling and I must go.
- John Muir

The mountains are, undeniably, the primary geological element of B.C., defining and directing so much of the British Columbia personality and experience. When you are to the west of them, you feel a line between you and the rest of the country—a line and a wall. The weather is different, the politics are different, the scenery is different. Yes, we Canadians have much in common, and I prefer to emphasize that, if I am emphasizing anything. But it's an unavoidable truth that there are regional differences, in this country and everywhere else too. In Canada, the Rocky Mountains are one of the explanations for those differences.

The trade-off is that they are so spectacular to look at, to play in, and to drive though.

We crossed into British Columbia near Golden, a lovely little town with a beautiful name. Behind me were the wheat fields and endless sky of the prairies, ahead was the much more varied countryside of this most western province and then the coast.

The natural landscape of this province reminds me of one of my favorite prescriptions for old age: happy, happy, happy, done. No decline, always looking forward, then good night. In B.C., you drive through mountain passes, hug the edges of emerald lakes, climb and descend, follow roads that curve left, right, and back again. Then just after Hope (another marvelous place name) you emerge from the mountains, make a straight shot for the lowland of the coast, following the river as it heads for open water, and then you're on the shore. Happy, happy, happy, done.

The essence of B.C. is nature. The tagline chosen by the government for numerous ads over the years is "supernatural B.C." and it is apt. Yes, B.C. is also known for wildlife, music, literature, languages (60 percent of the indigenous languages known in Canada have their origins here—that's about 32 languages and 59 dialects), painting, sports, agriculture (particularly wine), and natural resources (particularly trees). But it was the landscape, the places outside the cities, that filled me with wonder and left me remembering, long after I'd left.

I moved to Vancouver, the largest city in B.C., in 1981 and lived there until 2014. I had a job as the morning show host with CBC Radio, followed by a few years as the noon show open-line host, and then a newscaster. When I came to B.C., the population was about 2.5 million people; the latest figure is 4.6 million. Almost doubled. That makes the entire province about half the size of New York City, and about the size of Chicago and Houston combined. Vancouver and the cities around it in the Lower Mainland comprise about half the total population of the province. Are there American states with the same number of people as B.C.? Louisiana and Kentucky are close.

One of my first, and lasting impressions, on moving to the U.S. is that so many people live there. I knew it intellectually, of course; in Canada you grow up knowing that the neighbor next door is ten times your size. America is a huge country, physically, yes, but so is Canada. The thing is, though, you just don't have the people per square mile that there are in the States; sometimes it even feels like people per square inch, there! That impression has been reinforced during this nineteen-day drive across Canada; I knew it already, but if you ask me 'what's Canada got?' my from-the-gut answer is 'lots of room'. (My first answer only; see the last chapter of this book for a few more answers.)

'Lots of room' was not my first impression of Vancouver when I got there. Vancouver often makes newcomers feel claustrophobic. On a clear day, the mountains seem so close you can touch them. They crowd in on you and surround you. A rainy day is no better, with the dark sky seeming to be only five or six feet from the ground. The number of rainy days each year never falls below three digits, and averages 161 rainy days out of 365 (that's 44 percent!).

I was never one to feel claustrophobic in Vancouver—sometimes a bit low, maybe, but the rainy days often seemed cozy to me, too. If you're living your life and doing your work in a place, the weather is often less relevant to you than to the visitor who has three or four days to see a dozen sights, most of which are no fun if it's raining.

Vancouver has exactly as much 'room' as it needs, but you can't say it is underpopulated. The land space is limited. The ocean is under your nose and the mountains are at your back.

The city streets are extremely congested, thanks to a decision decades ago not to build freeways or perimeter roads. If you want to travel from the North Shore to downtown across Burrard Inlet, you have only two choices for the crossing: the Lions Gate Bridge and the Ironworkers' Memorial Bridge. It used to be that there were clearly delineated rush hours (although they began and ended earlier than you'd expect because of the three-hour time difference between Vancouver and the population centers in the East). If you could time your travel to midmorning you could hit the bridge at a slower time. But now there has been so much development, and there are so many people, that it's rush 'hour' all day long. The best thing to do is take a deep breath, relax, and just go with the flow.

If you've spent a lot of time in New York, Boston, Montréal, Hong Kong, London, Toronto, or any one of a dozen other traffic-packed cities, you might sniff and say the Vancouver traffic is a breeze. I give only my own reactions, comments and opinions here, and especially after northern Ontario and Newfoundland, I maintain that Vancouver traffic is *not* a breeze.

But I'm getting ahead of myself, rushing you to the coast when there is still the entire Interior to see. I crossed it in a day because that's the sort of trip I'm doing, but you could take far more time, as is the case in every one of the Canadian provinces.

After cruising through Golden, we let the car dance along twisty roads with majestic mountains on three sides. Kicking Horse Pass was the way through, and I couldn't help but be amazed by the incredibly high rocks surrounding the car. I let my mind be boggled by what a job it must have been to carve a road through that.

The rivers, creeks, and lakes beside the highway are usually emerald green, and that's one of the sights that first-time travelers through the Canadian Rockies often rave about. Not this time. Something about the effect of the smoke in the air from the forest fires was changing the perception of the color. The water levels looked very low, too.

Forest fires are a fact of life in British Columbia, but this was the worst wildfire season in six decades, we were told. Among the records broken: the most people evacuated, the largest area burnt in a single year, and the largest single fire. A state of emergency was declared in the province in July and continued through August to September 15. It was the first state of emergency in fourteen years and the longest in the province's history.

The weather on the morning of our drive across B.C. was rainy, mostly drizzle but sometimes big drops, significant water. This was a very twisty road with plenty of curves and spectacular scenery. I saw a sign that read "no passing lane for the next 3.7 km". Patience is a necessary characteristic for drivers in B.C.

I entertained myself for an hour or so by categorizing the passing styles of drivers on the highway. We have the "I've been sitting on your tail for five miles, now I'll make my move in the last two hundred yards before the passing lane disappears".

And then we have the "I'm not waiting that long for a passing lane, I'll just pull out now, and cross my fingers that there is no oncoming traffic until I'm done. Oh, there is? A massive tractor-trailer? Why don't you move over to the right? Or slow right down to let me by? I can't seem to find the accelerator . . . aaaaaahh—look out!. . ."

We reached Rogers Pass next. It is 1,400 meters at the summit, and my ears were popping for the past ten minutes on the way up. This was a phenomenal view and a phenomenal drive. Just imagine it with snow and ice! Not in the midst of a blizzard coming down, but afterwards, once the snow is a thick velvet blanket on everything and the tree branches have three or more inches of white frosting clinging to their needles. Beautiful.

Revelstoke is a place in the B.C. interior where they have dramatically geared up for tourists over the past fifteen years. I recalled passing this way in the eighties and nineties, and there wasn't nearly so much to see. At Three Valley Gap, the hotel with its red gables looked like something from a movie set in an alpine town. It's a stop for groups in tour buses and offers a Ghost Town in addition to the usual rooms, restaurants, and mountain views. We also saw signs for The Enchanted Forest, Crazy Creek Waterfall and Suspension Bridge, and MiniatureLand Camping (could be tiny campsites or could be best suited to petite people, didn't stop to find out).

The scenery through the Monashee Mountain range was spectacular. But I was finding the tight turns and the way the road hugged the mountain more than a little bit challenging and, whenever it was time for a meal, I was happy to stop and take a look around. The food was terrific; in B.C., I was offered Pacific salmon at every stop, prepared in various imaginative ways, often with an Asian flavor, and paired with world-class B.C. wines.

Other specialties in the B.C. cuisine category tend to cluster around seafood—mussels, oysters, crab, and prawns. Sustainable, locally grown food is a high priority in B.C., and we met people in quite a few restaurants who were pleased to tell us about the garden, the farm, or the fish boat where the ingredients for each dish were obtained. Chilliwack corn, Okanagan Valley fruit, traditional bannock, and, of course, Nanaimo bars, those scrumptious dessert concoctions of layers of wafers, custard, and melted chocolate, were all on the "to-do" list during this segment of the road trip.

We were still seeing and smelling the smoke from the forest fires from time to time and, along the banks of the Thompson River, I could see the damage—blackened trunks, countless empty spaces between the trees. Some of it was current and some went back years or even decades. Fires are a concern every summer, and this is one of the reasons that people in B.C. watch the weather so intently (as they do everywhere). Lightning strikes are one of the primary causes of fires. Rainfall—when, where, and how much of it—is as crucial for firefighters as it is for B.C. farmers.

At Kamloops, the air seemed better and one of the friendly people at the gas pumps told us that the day had been quite clear.

"But the day before was not," she said. "It's been totally unpredictable. It's the wind, you see. You just never know."

We turned south at Kamloops because we wanted to take Number 5, the Coquihalla Highway route, rather than stay on Highway 1, through the Fraser Canyon. The Coquihalla was built in the eighties; before then, the Fraser Canyon was the only option. You still can take that way, and if you're not in a hurry, you should. The views are spectacular everywhere, and the road is quite an experience. You're less likely to encounter transport trucks, too.

But the Fraser Canyon route is slower, and I was starting to smell the barn. Just like horses at the end of a day, heading for home and speeding up their pace as they got closer, I could feel myself leaning toward the west coast and that Mile Zero that was my target. I knew that the Coquihalla, the Kamloops to Merritt route, would let us put on the miles faster and get us there sooner. The Zig was onside.

This part of the drive took us off the mountain roads and into the valley. The Nicola Valley was one of my favorite areas of B.C. The gentle slopes, the colors of the rangelands, and the quality of light were unique, it seemed to me; but then, almost every place I see seems unique.

We passed many ranch driveways with 'statues' of cows out front. I saw one made of hay, with a cardboard 'face' and another of old tires painted with black spots on white, like a Holstein. As Zig and I pointed them out to one another, I took to calling it "ag art". We also passed herds of cows in the fields, lying down. Somehow the word 'herd' itself seemed to imply movement. Do you still call it a herd if they are lying down?

I also noticed the alpaca farms. They are such odd-looking animals, with their big, bulging eyes and long eyelashes.

I knew there was another mountain range to cross before we reached the Lower Fraser Valley near Vancouver, and I had my first sighting of the next rocky peak just past Little Fort and just before Clearwater. This town is renowned for whitewater rafting on the river in summer and for heli-skiing in winter.

The snow sheds on this part of the road were lit inside, making for a much less jittery passage through the rock. A snow shed looks a lot like a covered bridge. It's built as a sort of extension of a mountain slope and avalanches slide over the roof, leaving the road, railway or highway passable. Gates at either end of this section of highway are closed in winter if the snowfall is just too heavy, if the avalanche danger is high, if the mountain passes are closed, or if icy driving conditions make the highway just impossible.

This was hard to imagine on a day like today, top down on the car, with temperatures around 23 degrees Celsius (that's about 74 degrees Fahrenheit). The sun was shining on the roadside lakes and streams, making the water glisten, and a gentle wind was blowing through my hair.

You encounter this last series of mountains just before Hope, then drive out into the Fraser Valley at Chilliwack. It's so amazing to imagine these mountains once were an ocean floor, then raised through the action of many earthquakes, and now sinking again. From Chilliwack, the highway, straight and wide now, carried us on into Abbotsford, Fort Langley, Langley, Burnaby, and then Vancouver.

With every passing mile, the price of real estate climbed higher. Close to the coast, with the big views of the water and the sunsets, and the limited amount of land, the price per square foot went up like the wages of sin on Sunday. The price of a house or a condo is also sky-high in Toronto. Vancouver has changed a lot in the past thirty years and many people there now are used to the high cost of living they've seen elsewhere. Long-time Vancouverites and prairie dwellers eager to escape the frigid winters are usually shocked at the numbers.

It's expensive, but there are so many benefits, many of them intangible but no less valuable. Vancouver is a garden of culture, with art galleries, music venues, and performance spaces in abundance. Its music life has been enriched by the rock groups Chilliwack and Trooper, jazz man Lloyd Arntzen, Images in Vogue, Marianas Trench, Payolas, Skinny Puppy, Hedley, David Foster, and Doug and the Slugs. Artists Toni Onley, Jack Shadbolt, Bill Reid, and Emily Carr; writers George Bowering, Douglas Coupland, Malcolm Lowry, and W. P. Kinsella—have I left anybody out?

Of course, I have, but that's enough for now.

I had the map book open on my lap, looking for the best way to connect to Vancouver Island. The southern part of B.C. really is, geographically, the smallest part, and as I looked at the image as a whole I was impressed, once again, with just how much land and space there is. When you look at this map, you can't help but notice that part of the U.S., the state of Alaska, is w-a-a-a-a-y up north, with B.C. sandwiched in between. The stories of the creation of borders are fascinating. The back story is that the Americans bought Alaska from the Russians in 1867. (How much? $7.6 million.)

For a while, it looked as though the land in between might be absorbed into the American orbit, particularly during the California Gold Rush (1848 to 1855). About three hundred thousand people migrated to the gold fields to try their luck, most of them in 1849 (and they say that's the reason behind the nickname "forty-niners" for the fortune-hunters, and later for the football team). A lot of the prospectors traveled up and down what became the California-Oregon-Washington-B.C. coast, and there was a strong north–south pull and perspective.

But when gold was discovered in B.C., the British government in London began to take much more of an interest in the colony. The province was enticed into the Dominion of Canada when politicians requested a wagon road, so the story goes, and the British politicians responded with a promise of a national railroad, running from sea to sea. Oh, and they also promised to handle the province's existing debt. Exceed expectations, as they say. B.C. became the sixth province to join Confederation in 1871.

And, with that, the east–west orientation held sway and the seeds of my summer 2017 road trip were planted.

That night, the last one on this trip, was passed in Burnaby in a chain hotel attached to a casino. The price was right. The next morning it was off to Tsawwassen, to the B.C. ferry terminal to catch the boat to the province's capital city, Victoria, and the park that was to be the end of this road. Mile Zero.

The Trans-Canada Highway officially continues through Vancouver and across to the North Shore, into the village of Horseshoe Bay, where you would catch the ferry to Nanaimo on Vancouver Island. Just after World War II, when federal funding was allocated for highway-building, the decision was made to focus on connecting provincial capitals and major population centers. So the four-lane Island Highway 19, running south from Nanaimo to Victoria, got the attention and the Trans-Canada officially ends in Victoria.

There is a sign in Tofino, the village on the west coast of Vancouver Island, identifying it as the Western terminus of the Trans-Canada Highway. The Trans-Canada website says that sign went up in 1912, long before the actual decisions were made and the highway construction project started. Highway 4, from Qualicum Beach across the island to Tofino, is two lanes, steeply built with narrow shoulders. It's not a good choice for cyclists and not necessary if you want to drive from a Mile Zero marker to a Mile Zero marker. You would make your own choices, of course, but I figured that because we were staying at the south end of town, I wanted to ride the ferry from Tsawwassen to Victoria (a very scenic route through

Active Pass) and see the Butchart Gardens on the way into the city to find the marker. We could have finished off the trip by taking the other ferry route, too, from Horseshoe Bay to Nanaimo, then driving south down the island and going to the Gardens en route to the city, and maybe we'll do that next time.

That route is the better idea if you are in Whistler or Squamish. Whistler and the Blackcomb Mountains repeatedly take international prizes as ski resort destinations, and Whistler was Vancouver's partner in hosting the 2010 Winter Olympic Games.

This ferry ride was the fourth on my cross-Canada trip. It was not the shortest—that was the Englishtown ferry in Nova Scotia, which took less than five minutes and cost seven dollars. It was not the longest either—that label goes to the Newfoundland and Labrador crossing. The B.C. ferry trip was about an hour and a half, at a price of seventy-two dollars Canadian, with an extra ten dollars to make a reservation and ensure a parking spot on the boat.

This morning was the point on the trip when I realized I had underestimated the costs and underbudgeted. Does this happen to everybody? Credit card balances were growing and my ability to do math was shrinking. I crossed my fingers that we had enough to get home.

The sky was misty and gray as we set out on the final day of our journey. The wind was lively and, when we stood outside on the deck as the ferry pulled away from the dock, it was so gusty that I had to hold on. In August, I hadn't thought I'd need it, but at the last minute I brought a jacket and it was a good idea.

This part of the B.C. portion of the trip reminded me once again what an incredible variety of landscapes there are in this province, from mountains to valleys to small towns to big cities to rainforest to dessert.

We drove off the ferry and headed toward Victoria on Highway 17. We drove past wineries and farmers' markets, following the signs to The Butchart Gardens at Brentwood Bay. This was a phenomenal attraction, and I began to understand why people come from all over the world to see it. In the parking lot, I saw plates from New

Jersey (3,014 miles), Louisiana (2,587 miles), New Mexico (1,658 miles), Alaska (2,220 miles) and mine, from Georgia (2,945 miles). Road trippers, all. Do they park us in one place together?

The price to get in was thirty-two dollars Canadian and well worth it! I walked in past the Mediterranean Garden, the seeds and gift shop (will stop there on the way out), the cafeteria, the ice cream shop, the Dining Room and the massive, life-size chessboard.

The Butchart family began to build this amazing creation near Tod Inlet in 1904. Attracted there by the deposits of limestone needed for cement production, they built a factory and a business. Jennie Butchart decided to turn the limestone quarry into a sunken garden in 1909 and, over the years, a Japanese garden, an Italian Garden, a Rose Garden, and numerous other features were added. On this day in 2017 when I saw it, the fifty-five acres, tended by fifty-five gardeners and over five hundred staff, were in absolutely pristine condition.

I am not usually a fan of gardens, nor of internationally publicized tourist attractions, and I've been to Vancouver Island many times without checking out the Butchart Gardens.

I've wasted a lot of time.

It is completely worth the visit, partly for the jaw-dropping floral display and partly to share in the enjoyment of the others there. At one point, I met a young woman visitor standing near the rail who told me with great enthusiasm, and with no preamble, no 'hello, where are you from?', that I had to come to see it at Christmas time when it was all lit up. I saw one little two-year-old boy dashing around, just beaming. His dad said to me, as he chased the little guy, "He loves gardens." If the Butchart Gardens are his introduction to them, they will be a tough act to follow.

In the midst of the Sunken Garden, after you've walked a fair distance to get to it, you come upon the Ross Fountain, added in 1964 by the Butchart's grandson Ian Ross, to whom they gave the Gardens as a twenty-first birthday gift. The fountain was like a piece of music, with sprays of different shapes and size added one by one, until there was just an explosion of water.

We walked up a shady path to the Carousel, then past the Concert Lawn to the Rose Garden. A sign said it featured 2,500 varieties. How do they choose which ones to showcase?

I couldn't help but marvel at the work involved in maintaining something like this.

The Japanese Garden, farther down the path, has teahouses, bamboo groves, lily ponds, arches, a red wooden bridge, and a covered bridge with lanterns. At the back is a path to a view of the inlet, where they offer boat tours, historical pictures of the family and friends enjoying the property in summer, and a sensational view of the inlet.

Back up through the rest of the Japanese Garden, we came to the Star Fountain and then an archway cut through a formal hedge to the Italian Garden, the one Mr. Butchart liked best, we were told.

Mrs. Butchart had a private garden that you can see really well from the terrace of the Dining Room restaurant. This was my favorite, although the Japanese Garden was a close second. It had a roof of red, orange, and purple flowers, with white trellises supporting them. How do they keep everything so lush and vibrant? There was no sign of any one of the fifty-five gardeners to ask. When do they work, in the middle of the night?

In the Dining Room, they were offering High Tea in the English tradition—if you've never come across this before and want to try it, you'll find lots of opportunities in the Victoria area. They're very proud of their British history here in a city named for the British queen way back in 1843. Even though British Columbia's ethnic composition and English-as-a-first-language percentages have changed dramatically over the past century and a half, British traditions, imagery, and connections are still visible, even to the tourist just passing through.

On our way into Victoria, we also noticed a building boom, with cranes and new construction all over the downtown area. We were close to the finish line now, and the foot was starting to rest a little heavy on the accelerator pedal as we got closer to Mile Zero. Even the car could smell the barn. The tourist traffic was heavy, though, and there was no zipping through these last few miles.

Meandering through Victoria, along Douglas Street to the waterfront, we found Beacon Hill Park. Mile Zero is in a quiet place at the water's edge. We parked, walked across the grass, and . . . done.

There was the Mile Zero marker! We took our photographs and walked around for a while, looking at the tribute to Terry Fox. We also found a reference to Steve Fonyo, another Canadian living with cancer who ran cross-country to raise funds and awareness, and to Al Howie, a long-distance runner who made his epic effort to raise awareness for people with mental health challenges. Canadians seem to like going coast to coast, across that wide expanse. I can relate.

Mark Twain wrote "Twenty years from now you will be more disappointed by the things you didn't do than by the ones you did do. So throw off the bowlines, sail away from the safe harbor. Catch the trade winds in your sails. Explore. Dream. Discover."

That night, after celebrating the end of the road trip in Victoria with B.C. wines, local produce, and cheese, we watched the lights on the B.C. Parliament Buildings, home to the Legislative Assembly. I felt as though we'd really followed Mark Twain's advice. The Zig brought out a red marker bought especially for the occasion and drew a red line across our paper map of Canada. I took a photograph.

The next day we stopped by a bookstore and bought a guidebook to Route 66.

Some famous people born in, educated in, housed or claimed by B.C.?
Actor Michael J. Fox. Wheelchair athlete and fundraiser extraordinaire Rick Hansen. Jazz singer Diana Krall. Singer, songwriter, and artist Joni Mitchell. Olympic athlete Nancy Greene. Singer Michael Bublé. Spiritual teacher Eckhart Tolle. Singer Bryan Adams. Actress Kim Cattrall. Basketball player Steve Nash. Businessman Jim Pattison. Canadian icon Terry Fox.

What to see next time?
I'd like to go north and see the Bowron Lakes area, maybe do some canoeing. I've never seen Haida Gwaii and the northern B.C. coast, and I would particularly like to visit the totem poles there that inspired painter Emily Carr.

What to see more of?
The B.C. Interior, with clear skies and unthreatened trees. The Okanagan wine country.

What to see less of?
Burned forests, smoky air, and fewer people facing heavy losses.

Surprises?
Hard to find these, when I lived there for thirty-three years.
But . . . That the lights at night on Grouse Mountain glowed even brighter than I remembered and that the sunsets over English Bay had become even more spectacular. Hadn't thought that was even possible.

Chapter Eleven

REFLECTIONS

I started out with the title Rumble Strip as an idea for a perspective to take on this journey. (It is going to be a series, by the way, with accounts of travels off the Interstate on interesting side roads in the U.S. next in the plan. Manuscripts on emotionally evocative literary landmarks and small places that celebrate Christmas in strange and wonderful ways are also underway.)

Slow down, take a look around, stay on track and alert. Canada 150 summed up my destination, my reason for going now, and the realization of a lifelong dream to cross it by road from one edge to the other.

But now that the trip is over, I've realized that the title also described the sort of experience or fresh knowledge that other travel writers have described. A sort of thunderbolt or epiphany, coming from the ground instead of the sky. But not an earthquake, more of a gentle rumble.

I don't think that, over the three weeks, I had any sort of earth-shaking or life-changing epiphany or realization. But I did have numerous moments of being stirred to look more carefully and to think more deeply about Canada and its places.

Coming back was like coming home and, right from the first moments to the north of the border crossing in New Brunswick, I felt familiar and comfortable. I didn't expect that the years living in America had changed me, particularly. I didn't expect to feel strange, back in Canada, and I didn't. Perhaps at another time, the epiphany will be that I **have** changed; perhaps I just haven't been away long enough. But I think as soon as you start trying to anticipate what the epiphany will be, by definition, it can't be an epiphany any more—it has become just what you already knew. It has to be a complete surprise (although what an incomplete surprise is, I couldn't tell you).

On this trip, as I've said, I didn't have one. But maybe epiphanies can be delayed. Maybe six months or a year from now, I will realize that I expected one thing, thought I'd seen it, and was suddenly hit by another, radically different, life-changing thought. We'll see.

I learned a few things that I don't think are momentous enough to qualify as epiphanies but still were lessons worth noting. For example, all the worrying I had done about advance booking and planning was a waste of energy. So often, the anxiety that we feel comes from the input of other people, each of whom has his or her own point of view and departure. The tourism departments of whatever province could probably tell me hundreds of stories of visitors who'd been disappointed in their plans to see a particular attraction because they hadn't realized they needed to book a seat in a certain way, on a certain day of the week, or through a certain route. So they pushed for months and months of advance notice and commitment and had me in a spasm of insecurity over whether I'd screwed up everything by not thinking far enough ahead of time.

As we already know, it all turned out just fine. For example, we had ferry transportation to the Rock and back with little to no trouble. I didn't need a six-month planning window. I hesitate to recommend that you ignore all the (very solid) advice given by the official government websites, the travel advisor sites, the scenic swamis, and the going gurus, and I hereby issue all the required legalese that says I take no responsibility for any changes in details that may or may not have led you to make plans based on my plans that left you without a ticket, a plate, a bed, or a place to sit down. Make your own plans, you shortcut-seeker!

I didn't book months in advance, but I was willing to take what was offered, without complaint, and I kept my expectations very low, knowing that I was slipping in through a side door, metaphorically. I discovered that you don't have to do exactly what they say, and you don't have to know every detail before you get there. I'm just sayin'.

One of my favorite thoughts about travel comes from novelist Aldous Huxley, who wrote "to travel is to discover that everyone is wrong about other countries." Your Canada would not be my Canada. My U.S. would not be your U.S. Everyone has their own opinion and reaction; people waste far too much effort and energy on trying to convince others, and it just can't be done.

So, without any thought of trying to convince you of anything about Canada, here are some of the conclusions I reached after my most recent three weeks there:

The country was more unified than it has been in any decade past, and people shared more of a collegial spirit. Regardless of recent political events or divisions based on past injustice, Canada seemed to me to have more community, more interconnection than in previous times. I don't think this had anything to do with an arbitrary date on a calendar or with anything magical about 150 years, and I don't know what the cause might be.

I recall that in the seventies Canada had what was often described as an 'inferiority complex', its nose pressed up against the glass of the border, watching all the glamorous and world-defining events that took place in America. I think those days have long passed, and that Canada has nothing about which to feel slower or smaller. It has its unique and invaluable character, its inimitable beauty, and its devoted people. I knew that, about Canada, before I began this trip; all of the expectations I had of national pride and regional differentiation were met. But in addition, I felt calm and confidence. Yes, on the surface, in certain places you could point to economic whitecaps or political chop, but beneath the surface, running deep, Canada is an ocean.

Once the miles were behind us, I was faced with the question of whether to add more. Having driven all the way from east coast to west, was it a good idea to turn around and drive back? Or, if not a good idea, at least a slightly intriguing one? I'd certainly have no trouble finding new roads to explore, and there would be a certain satisfying symmetry about swinging a bit south and then driving back across the U.S. I know that for some the idea of a three-week road trip is just torture—more than thirty minutes in a car and they are hoping to hang themselves from boredom, restlessness, or irritation at the other drivers. Not me. I would do it over and over; the phrase 'road trip' has me with my hand on the doorknob, ready to go.

But I wasn't sure I had the capacity or the attention span for another three weeks in the car, just now. The business needed attention; plus, I was eager to get down on paper all the observations and thoughts I had about what I'd already seen. I also wasn't sure the car had the capacity or the stamina for another five thousand miles, without some serious time and coin spent in the shop.

So the convertible was sold and the tickets bought. We got back by flying—another kind of fun and a visual feast. Not better, just different. Nothing will replace a good road trip. The next one is already in the planning stages.

CANADA 150 PLAYLIST

This is some of the music I listened to on this journey. The choices are those of a fan.
You can follow the playlist on Spotify by searching Canada150.RumbleStripBooks.DJG.

You can also find there the names of the albums where each of the songs is to be found, should you decide you want to buy and hear the artist's entire context for the piece.

This list of one hundred songs is organized east to west, by province, after beginning with two of my four favorite Canadian songs. The other two bookend the list.

It's neither complete nor comprehensive, and is completely subjective. You might enjoy hearing them in geographic order and so I've included the provincial reference (although there are quite a few artists who are claimed by more than one province, and my decision to include them in an particular spot is also completely subjective).
You also might just put them on a shuffle.

Thank you to all these songwriters and musicians for everything they've done to make all of our lives better and our experience of our country deeper.

Canada
Life is a Highway   Tom Cochrane
A Case of You   Joni Mitchell

Newfoundland
I'se the B'y   Great Big Sea
Consequence Free   Great Big Sea

Run Run Away	Great Big Sea
Walk on the Moon	Great Big Sea
Four-Stop Jigs	Figgy Duff
"Rose"	*Titanic*
In the Bar/Heave Away	*Come from Away*
The Banks of Newfoundland	Paul McKenna Band
Ordinary Day	Great Big Sea
Rattlin' Bog	Irish Descendants

Nova Scotia

Farewell to Nova Scotia	Ian and Sylvia
Barrett's Privateers	Stan Rogers
Northwest Passage	Stan Rogers
Home I'll Be	Rita MacNeil
Mairi's Wedding	The Rankin Family
Reels from Fiddle Music 101	Ashley MacIsaac
I Wouldn't Want to Lose Your Love	April Wine
Snowbird	Anne Murray
Angel	Sarah MacLachlan
Farewell to the Rhonda	Men of the Deeps

Prince Edward Island

The Hockey Song	Stompin' Tom Connors
Bud the Spud	Stompin' Tom Connors
Les Deux Johns	Barachois
Don Messer Tribute	Peter Solmes
He Wrote Too Many Songs about His Girlfriend	Nancy White
Atlantic Blue	Tara MacLean
Happy Baby	Tara MacLean
If It's All Right with You	written by Gene MacLellan, sung by CatherineMacLellan
The Call	Written by Gene MacLellan
I'm a River	Jenn Grant

New Brunswick

Garder le Feu	Roch Voisine
Hélène	Roch Voisine
I Wouldn't Dance	David Myles
Change My Mind	David Myles

Inner Ninja — Classified (feat. David Myles)
I Don't Want to be Alone — Ken Tobias
Alberta Gold — Matt Andersen
Weightless — Matt Andersen

Québec
Brother Down — Sam Roberts Band
Bridge to Nowhere — Sam Roberts Band
Dance Me to the End of Love — Leonard Cohen
Hallelujah — Leonard Cohen
Te v'la — Robert Charlebois
Quebec Love — Robert Charlebois
Because You Loved Me — Celine Dion
Encore un Soir — Celine Dion
Mon Pays — Gilles Vigneault
Dis-moi — Monique Leyrac
We Used to Wait — Arcade Fire

Ontario
Hold On, We're Going Home — Drake
Early Morning Rain — Gordon Lightfoot
Wherefore and Why — Gordon Lightfoot
Starboy — The Weeknd
Baby — Justin Bieber
That Don't Impress Me Much — Shania Twain
5 Days in May — Blue Rodeo
Bobcaygeon — Tragically Hip
Complicated — Avril Lavigne
If I Had $1,000,000 — Barenaked Ladies
Big Bang Theory Theme — Barenaked Ladies
Hats Off to the Stranger — Lighthouse
Put Your Head on my Shoulder — Paul Anka
Harvest Moon — Neil Young
For What It's Worth — Buffalo Springfield (with Neil Young)
Our House — Crosby, Stills, Nash & Young
Suite Judy Blue Eyes — Crosby, Stills, Nash & Young

You Made Me So Very Happy	Blood, Sweat and Tears

Manitoba

Shakin' All Over	The Guess Who (Chad Allan and the Expressions)
No Sugar Tonight	The Guess Who
Runnin' Back to Saskatoon	The Guess Who
Superman's Song	Crash Test Dummies
You Ain't Seen Nothing Yet	Bachman Turner Overdrive
The Cat Came Back	Fred Penner
Before You	Chantal Kreviazuk
Timeless Love	Burton Cummings
One Last Sundown	Doc Walker

Saskatchewan

Carey	Joni Mitchell
Free Man in Paris	Joni Mitchell
Big Yellow Taxi	Joni Mitchell
The Circle Game	Joni Mitchell
The Last Saskatchewan Pirate	Tyler Lewis
Until It's Time for You to Go	Buffy Sainte-Marie

Alberta

Insensitive	Jann Arden
How You Remind Me	Nickelback
Four Strong Winds	Ian & Sylvia
Sweet City Woman	The Stampeders
Throw Your Hands Up	Stereos
Crying	k.d.lang (duet with Roy Orbison)

B.C.

Too Bad	Doug and the Slugs
Everything	Michael Bublé
Haven't Met You Yet	Michael Bublé
Summer of '69	Bryan Adams
18 Till I Die	Bryan Adams
Call Me Maybe	Carly Rae Jepsen
On the Sunny Side of the Street	Diana Krall
You Don't Know Me	Diana Krall (duet with Ray Charles)

Canada
Share The Land   The Guess Who
Canadian Railroad Trilogy   Gordon Lightfoot

GAIL HULNICK

ABOUT THE AUTHOR

Gail Hulnick is a former broadcast journalist who now divides her time between the United States and Canada. Her other books include mystery novels *The Lion's Share of the Air Time*, *A Bird in the Sand*, *Resorting to Murder*, and *Resorting to Larceny*.

ABOUT RUMBLE STRIP BOOKS

Rumble Strip Books are published by The WindWord Group Publishing & Media, as part of its Sirocco Press imprint. Beginning with Canada 150, each of these travel memoirs features a personal journey over noteworthy roads in an interesting car. Coming soon . . . twisty U.S. backroads, literary landmarks, holiday road trips, a BMW 330 Ci, a C3 Corvette and an Aston Martin DB11.

www.ingramcontent.com/pod-product-compliance
Lightning Source LLC
Chambersburg PA
CBHW071621080526
44588CB00010B/1219